WHAT THEY NEVER TOLD US

True Stories of Family Secrets and Hidden Identities Revealed

GAIL LUKASIK

Skyhorse Publishing

Skyhorse Publishing books may be purchased in bulk at special discounts for sales promotion, corporate gifts, fund-raising, or educational purposes. Special editions can also be created to specifications. For details, contact the Special Sales Department, Skyhorse Publishing, 307 West 36th Street, 11th Floor, New York, NY 10018 or info@skyhorsepublishing.com.

Skyhorse® and Skyhorse Publishing® are registered trademarks of Skyhorse Publishing, Inc.®, a Delaware corporation.

Visit our website at www.skyhorsepublishing.com.

Please follow our publisher Tony Lyons on Instagram @tonylyonsisuncertain

10 9 8 7 6 5 4 3 2 1

Library of Congress Control Number: 2024945075

Cover design by Kai Texel
Cover photographs by Getty Images

Print ISBN: 978-1-5107-8018-7
Ebook ISBN: 978-1-5107-8113-9

Printed in the United States of America

Once again, to my husband, Jerry.

"The wrong things are kept secret."
—Photographer and activist, Nan Goldin

CONTENTS

Epilogue

WHAT THEY NEVER TOLD US

CHAPTER 1

A Social and Scientific Phenomenon

"My mother always said there were some things that should remain secret, and that people may be hurt if things are made public."
—*Email from Sandra C., May 14, 2022*

FAMILY SECRETS ARE NO LONGER REMAINING SECRET. ADVANCES IN SCIENCE and technology have far outpaced our ability to deal with the consequences of these family discoveries regarding parentage and/or race and ethnicity. Adoptions, non-paternal events (NPE), donor conceptions, and hidden racial heritages are being revealed at an increasing rate.

In part, what's fueling these unexpected and disorienting discoveries are the proliferation of consumer DNA tests and easy access to genealogy websites, such as Ancestry.com, 23andMe, and MyHeritage.

As of 2019, approximately 26 million Americans have taken a consumer DNA test, about two out of ten people. Since then, it's estimated that number has increased, exceeding over 100 million. Of those 100 million-plus people, about four in ten (38 percent) have had unexpected familial results.[1] And that's not counting the other family members, parents and siblings, who also are impacted by these surprises.

Behind these numbers is devastating trauma, which tears families apart and often leaves the discoverer, or the "family secret," stranded and isolated. Ancestry, recognizing the increase in unexpected discoveries, has a warning in their privacy statement: "You may discover unexpected facts about yourself or your family when using our services. Once discoveries are made, we can't undo them."[2]

Not only are they irreversible, they also leave the discoverers feeling betrayed. Repeatedly, the people I interviewed for this book expressed their feelings of being betrayed by a parent or parents who kept their biological identities from them. When they learned that their parents had lied to them, that sacred bond between them and their parents was shattered. Their trauma was amplified by their family's inability to understand the impact of the secret, telling them it doesn't matter and that they're still the same person.

But to the discoverer, it does matter. And they're not the same person anymore.

Late discovery adoptee Brad Ewell from Chapter 13 explained, "It absolutely matters when you wake up one day and you find out you're not the kid of the people who raised you. It's three years now and I still struggle with it."

Unexpected parentage is not the only surprise people who take consumer DNA tests experience. Many also find out that their race or ethnicity is different than what they were told—a shift that in some cases challenges their ideas about minorities and religion.

As Libby Copland points out in *The Lost Family*, these identity changing discoveries force you to rethink what you've known about race and religion, about your place in the family and your role in the world.[3]

Besides DNA tests, family secrets are also revealed by family members in times of extreme emotional stress, as if the secret keeper can no longer remain quiet.

Robin from Chapter 19 learned she was donor-conceived during a heated argument with her mother.

"I don't know why I bothered with all that trouble to be artificially inseminated to have you," her mother shouted at her.

Robin said, "That shut me up."

Besides shutting her up, her mother's shocking revelation left her questioning her very existence.

With the rise of these unexpected revelations, there's been a subsequent rise in support groups and organizations to help people cope with these identity shattering discoveries, from offering moral support to helping find birth parents.

The first summit to bring together these disparate groups—adoptees, donor conceived, and those conceived through a non-paternal event (NPE)—was held in 2023. The summit offered panels and workshops, such as, "The Impact of Growing Up with Secrets & Lies," "Ethnicity Shifts from a DNA Surprise," and "Ethics & Human Rights in our Origins," to name a few.

But despite the overwhelming number of people affected by these life-altering discoveries, the lack of treatment and research is shocking. Little has been done on a professional level to examine the emotional and psychological impact of betrayal, deception, and finding out that you're not who your parents told you you were.

The American Psychological Association still has no protocol for assessing and working with a Misattributed Parentage Experience (MPE) client/patient. Or anyone whose identity has been broken.

Josephine, PhD Psychologist, from Chapter 10, has made parent discovery her area of expertise.

"I had to teach my therapist why I needed therapy on this issue. It's so easily dismissed by a surprisingly large number of clinicians," Josephine said.

As Debbie Kennett, Researcher and Genetic Genealogist, University College, London, states: [There's a] great need for research into the cultural and personal impact of DNA testing and the secrets it uncovers."[4]

The first step toward understanding the impact of uncovered family secrets is to give them a voice.

What They Never Told Us tells the stories of ordinary people who made extraordinary, life-changing discoveries about their parentage and/or race and ethnicity that shattered their identities.

From the Texas policeman who discovered his biological father is a murderer; to the Seattle CEO who suffered for her Black identity only to find out she isn't Black; to the Chicago area high school guidance counselor who suddenly had forty-nine half-siblings—these stories and the others in *What They Never Told Us* sit at the forefront of a changing social landscape we've yet to understand or cope with—challenging our notions of identity, race, ethnicity, and what constitutes a family in the twenty-first century.

Blending social history and personal narratives, each story delves into the devastating psychological trauma of uncovering a hidden family secret with all the twists and turns of a mystery novel from how the discovery was made, to why it was kept secret, to the arduous, sometimes disappointing, quest to find the biological parent or parents.

To fully understand the secrecy surrounding these family secrets, the book examines pre-WWII and post-WWII attitudes toward infertility, adoption, donor conception, race and racial passing, and unmarried pregnant women.

Prefacing these harrowing narratives is my own confusing and sometimes painful journey to redefine my racial identity after the publication of my memoir, *White Like Her: My Family's Story of Race and Racial Passing*, which thrust me into the public spotlight of public opinion.

All the interviewees have given me permission to share their stories. Some have chosen to use a pseudonym.

PART 1

Race, Ethnicity, and Identity

CHAPTER 2

My Racial Discovery Journey

In 1995, while scrolling through the 1900 Louisiana census records, I made a startling discovery. My paternal grandfather, Azemar Frederic, and his family had been designated as Black by the state of Louisiana. On the census records, a B had been written behind each of their names for race.

It's hard to describe the shock I felt that day sitting in front of the microfilm machine in the dark basement of the Buffalo Grove Family History Center, a headache building behind my eyes after hours of looking through census records for my elusive grandfather. A man that my mother claimed to know little to nothing about—no birth or death date, no photographs. He was my mystery man.

Maybe B doesn't mean Black, I told myself. Maybe the census taker made a mistake. After all, he'd designated my grandfather's sex as female.

Wanting clarification, I asked the thinly precise, gray-haired woman who was helping people with the microfilm if B meant Black.

"Oh, yes," she said. "B is for Black."

Then she launched into a slew of racial slurs using the N word repeatedly—"niggers in every woodshed," "nigger babies' candy"—ending her racial rant with a declaration of my heritage, "You're the one with the slaves in your family."

During her racial attack, she chuckled as if it were all a joke that I was in on.

It was my first, but not my last, experience of racism aimed at me.

I left the center shaken. I couldn't get out of there fast enough. Though it was a cold January afternoon, I sat in my car not able to drive home.

What had just happened?

As I stated in my book, *White Like Her: My Family's Story of Race and Racial Passing*: "In a split second I became someone else, my identity in question. When I walked into the squat, brown building I was a white woman. When I left, I didn't know who I was . . . I couldn't get out of my head that I wasn't who I thought I was. I wasn't this white woman. Or I was this white woman who was also this Black woman. Or I was neither? Who was I really? And what did my racial mixture mean?"[5]

When I pulled out of the history center's driveway, I glanced at myself in the rearview mirror. Nothing in my appearance had changed. Yet everything had changed. I clung to the hope that the census taker had made a mistake. That the racist woman was mistaken.

At the suggestion of my friend Linda Landis Andrews, who discovered as an adult that she was adopted, I wrote to the state of Louisiana as my mother requesting a copy of her birth certificate.

This will settle it, I thought.

Her birth certificate left me more confused. For race, there were three letters in parenthesis: *col.* I reminded myself that in 1921 Jim Crow laws were in effect, which meant one drop of African blood made you "colored."

Linda told me to write another letter to the state. "Who knows what 'col' meant back then?"

The state's letter left no confusion about the meaning of "col."

"The use of the term 'colored' has been ambiguous over time, however, did become more closely associated with the Black race."[6]

Although I desperately wanted to talk to my mother about her birth certificate and the 1900 census designation of the Frederics as Black, fate intervened. Shortly after my discovery, my father was diagnosed with throat cancer. It wasn't the right time.

Two years after my initial discovery, I was finally able to ask my mother about her racial heritage. When I look back on that day, I realize how different my life would have been if my mother had reacted differently. If she hadn't sworn me to secrecy until her death, saying, "How will I hold my head up with my friends if they know?"

If she had discussed her life-changing decision to pass as white, explained to me why she did it, how she accomplished it, what her fears were, and how she was able to transform herself, I wouldn't have appeared on PBS's *Genealogy Roadshow* in 2015. I would have known who she truly was and who I truly was. Her refusal to talk left me without answers about my racial identity.

But if I hadn't appeared on *Genealogy Roadshow*, I wouldn't have discovered my mother's lost family, which led to my writing *White Like Her*, and attaining national and international notoriety.

*   *   *

After the book's publication, I wrote an article about my mother's story for *The Washington Post's Inspired Life* section, "My mother spent her life passing as white. Discovering her secret changed my view of race." I also wrote articles for *The Daily Beast*, *Salon.com*, and *mic.com*.

In the *Washington Post* article, I declared my racial identity.

"But although I could check 'other' or 'multiracial' when asked my race on a form, I still identify as a white woman. At this late point, it would be disingenuous of me to claim any other identity. I've enjoyed white privilege my entire life."[7]

I had no idea what a flashpoint my claiming a white identity would become as my mother's story and my racial identity came under the glare of public scrutiny.

As a result of my *Washington Post* article, Kate Uebergang, the producer for the *Megyn Kelly Today Show*, contacted me. She wanted to book me and my newly found family—Cousin Stephanie and Uncle Fred on the show. She told me that the day my article appeared in the *Washington Post*, the lead story concerned Kevin Spacey. She asked herself what would have been the lead article if not for him? It was my story.

Arrangements were made, a date set, February 5, 2018. I could hardly believe my good fortunate. For a writer, appearing on a national television show is the equivalent of winning the lottery.

Though I didn't know it at the time, my appearance on the *Megyn Kelly Today Show* would change my life in ways I couldn't have predicted.

CHAPTER 3

The *Megyn Kelly Today Show*

"You sold your family for 30 pieces of silver."
—*Anonymous email received after my appearance*
on The Megyn Kelly Today Show

TREMBLING WITH EXCITEMENT, I WAIT IN THE WINGS OF STUDIO 6A, WATCHing a stagehand lead my newly-discovered relatives—Cousin Stephanie Frederic and Uncle Fred (Azemar Frederic) to their front row seats.

We are about to appear on *The Megyn Kelly Today Show*—live.

For what seemed like hours, we were sequestered in the aptly named green room, Cuba, (one of our ancestors immigrated from Cuba to New Orleans in the nineteenth century) and feted with a generous platter of food and non-alcoholic beverages. None of which I touched—too nervous. Then we were whisked off to hair and makeup before being called backstage.

None of it feels real.

Last night over dinner at the Club Quarters Hotel's restaurant, The

Terrace, we once again marveled at the miracle of finding each other. Saying nothing about the years lost because of racism's ugly legacy.

Unlike my appearance on PBS's *Genealogy Roadshow* three years ago, where my mother's family mystery was solved with certainty, there are no mysteries to be solved this morning. I know who I am.

At least, that's what I think

"Gail." I turn. Megyn Kelly walks toward me. Urban chic in her herringbone skirt, red silky blouse, and spiky black boots.

Though I'm aware of her dubious reputation as a former news commentator on *Fox News*, Kate Eubergang, her producer with the charming British accent, assured me that Megyn is rebranding herself with a softer image. Though I'm unclear what that means, I'm about to find out.

However, in a few months, her attempt at rebranding will disintegrate when she makes an insensitive remark about wearing black face for Halloween, forcing her to resign from *The Today Show*.

But right now, I'm not thinking of Kelly's rebranded image.

Since I learned I was to be on the show, I've been in a state of near apoplexy that refuses to leave me, robbing me of sleep, obsessively practicing my answers to possible questions. My anxiety is so rampant, I've been avoiding touching public door knobs and the escalator belt at our local shopping mall for fear of catching a cold.

"I really enjoyed your book," Megyn says as a way of introduction.

I thank her, wondering if she's even read it. *Always the skeptic.*

She's shorter than I imagined—petite, strikingly pretty with loose blond curls.

Again, that feeling of unreality washes over me.

Since the publication of *White Like Her* and my article in *The Washington Post*, my personal and professional life have become public, leaving me teetering between vulnerable and delighted. As a mid-list mystery author who's enjoyed modest success, I welcomed the publicity. But as I was about to discover, I'm ill-prepared for the spotlight and the harsh scrutiny that comes with it.

"How do you pronounce your last name?" Megyn asks.

I tell her. She smiles then walks into the brightly lit studio and introduces my story.

A video unrolls. It's the video that was filmed at my home a few days earlier. My mind spins elsewhere, suddenly seeing the enlarged 1950s photographs of my parents and me plastered on the back wall of the studio where a select audience sits. They will be behind me during my interview, their reactions to my story part of the show.

In the photographs, my parents are so young, so full of promise.

A sudden rush of emotion shakes me, bringing me to tears.

Get a grip, don't cry, I tell myself.

I take in a deep breath to calm my emotions and remember what Gail Grasso, the producer who came to my house for the initial interview, told me. "The actual live show goes very fast. Try and enjoy it."

But it's impossible for me not to be moved by the photos. In one my mom and I are posed in front of a 1940s black car. I'm maybe four, my brother not on the scene yet. My mom cradles me in her arms. I want her arms around me now.

"Are you pleased, Mom?" I ask her.

I can't help but feel that I've broken my vow to her once again in a very public way. Even though technically I haven't. My promise not to tell her racial secret ended four years ago with her death in 2014. I'd faithfully kept her promise for seventeen years, carrying her shame and fear out of loyalty and love.

In a few minutes I'll sit on that stage in the royal blue, velvet chair and tell 2.4 million viewers my mother's story of passing as a white woman, of my vow to keep her secret until her death, and how after her death I appeared on PBS's *Genealogy Roadshow*, which led to my finding the family she never knew.

Later Uncle Fred and Cousin Stephanie will join me on stage and tell their story of family discovery. How they didn't know I existed. How my mother's passing as white severed the Frederic family tree and left two branches unknown to each other—illustrating the destructive power of racism and family secrets.

The tape ends. There's a commercial break. I'm called to the stage.

After the commercial ends, Megyn Kelly says, "We're joined now by Gail Lukasik who's written about her mother's secret past in her book *White Like Her*. Welcome, Gail."

Gail Grasso is right. The interview goes fast. Though it's impossible to enjoy it. I'm asked uncomfortable questions about my father's bigotry, my mother's quirky habits, and her refusal to talk about her passing as white.

I repeat her shocking response when I confronted her with her racial secret—a response that always makes me uneasy in its subtle racism, what growing up in the Jim Crow south did to my mother's sense of self.

"You can't tell anyone. How will I hold my head up with my friends?" she begged me.

Then, Kelly leans in and asks the question that will cause a seismic shift I never expected or could have prepared for, setting me again on a path of racial uncertainty and woundedness.

"How do you identify?" Kelly asks.

It's not the first time I've been asked this question nor will it be the last. But, it's the first time I've been asked in front of a national audience.

In the five months after the book's release, I settled on an answer that I believe reflects my white cultural upbringing and is sensitive to African Americans who've experienced racism, never questioning if my answer really defines me. In my naivete about race and my need to please, I believe no one could be offended by my answer. I'm not Rachel Dolezal boldly claiming she's Black when she was genetically white.

"I'm a white woman with Black heritage," I state confidently.

Then, hoping to move past this need to racially label, I add, "I consider race a social construct."

It's the same answer I gave a few months earlier at a St. Louis bookstore when an African American woman, who identified herself as a member of the St. Louis Black Caucus, asked about my racial identity.

She smiled at my answer, saying that's what she wanted to hear. And that any other answer would have been wrong. Though I didn't know what a wrong answer would have been, I felt like I dodged a racial bullet.

The questions continue. Another commercial break.

Uncle Fred and Cousin Stephanie are called to the stage. Stephanie sits beside me. "You did good," she whispers.

Their presence soothes me. I did good. I've been embraced by my "lost" family.

I'll soon learn not everyone thought I did good.

CHAPTER 4

Black People Shouldn't Read This Book

TWO WEEKS AFTER MY APPEARANCE ON *THE MEGYN KELLY TODAY SHOW*, AN African American woman skewers me on Amazon.

"Black people shouldn't read this book," she advises.

Television is an unpredictable friend.

Because of the *Today Show* appearance, *White Like Her* skyrockets to the #1 book on Amazon. I receive a request from Redglass Pictures to be in their documentary film, *History of Memory*, as well as invitations from countless other well-known television shows, BBC World News Service and CBC Canada, as well as inquiries from film producers. While I'm amazed and grateful, I'm troubled by this woman's comments.

She's not going to read my book, because I identified as a white woman with Black ancestry. She doesn't understand why white people make such a big deal out of discovering Black ancestry. It won't be the last time I hear that criticism.

What really affects me is her contention that I'm holding on to the concept of being a white woman. She finds that offensive. My identifying as a white woman with Black heritage is a betrayal of my Black ancestry.

At least read the book, I fume. *If you read it, you'd see that my Black ancestry is revered. I give voice to my ancestors who had no voice, showing how racism affected their lives.*

A feeling of hopelessness washes over me. How can we ever bridge the divide between the races if we don't listen to each other?

I'm angry, bewildered, and wounded. I ask two of my friends to write counter reviews on Amazon. They do.

But it doesn't assuage the sting of her comments. As a writer, I'm blessed and cursed with a writer's sensitivity and need to question. I wonder if there's some truth in what she said?

In my effort to be sensitive to African Americans who've suffered racism, did I betray my Black ancestry by not fully embracing it publicly?

Comparing this woman's Amazon review to the St. Louis Black Caucus woman's response, it becomes painfully clear to me that other people want to define my racial identity. And if I don't identify as they think I should, they take offense.

I can hear my mother saying, "See, this is why I didn't tell anybody. Why I vowed you to secrecy. I was trying to protect you."

Though I never faulted my mother for passing as white, I do fault her for not talking to me about it, for not sharing her decision with me, for leaving me rootless and adrift, clinging to one identity because I was never told I had another.

Her silence was never the answer. Breaking it was.

I don't answer the woman on Amazon. But her comments stay with me, always there lurking when I'm questioned in public about my racial identity.

My national appearance on *The Today Show* also has another unexpected effect. It unleashed an avalanche of emails from strangers from around the world, desperate to share their own family secrets—some racial, some parental—all life altering. The catalyst for many of these unimagined surprises was a consumer DNA test. Though I didn't know it then, a social and scientific phenomenon was occurring that no one could have predicted or was prepared for.

On the advice of my publicist, I set up a separate account to answer the barrage of emails. Many of them begin with the same words, "I haven't told anyone."

Then they tell me, a total stranger, what their families have kept hidden. The details are intimate and heartfelt. They've chosen me to be the repository of their deepest secrets, all because I shared on national television my family's racial secret. It's as if a door has been opened for them, allowing them entry to a room where they feel safe and understood.

I'm struck by an email from South Africa that succinctly expresses the dilemma faced by mixed race people who can pass as white.

> *Thank you for sharing your perspective on the brutal yoke society places on "White" Coloureds. Stay Coloured and you will most likely stay broke and broken. Play "White" and you have access to the better life—but you stay broken . . . Continue to tell the story of your late mother's anguish. It is a story repeated and hidden in thousands of homes.* —R. Harris

Sometimes the emails tear at my heart with their longing for family:

> *Your story resembles my crazy passing story. I was adopted and told I was Puerto Rican, but found out later from my birth certificate that my father was Negro. . . . I wish I could find my father and know the story of my Black heritage, so that is why I'm contacting you. Maybe you know of some resources to help me find my father.* –J. Allen

I tell her how I found my grandfather and the truth of our family's history. I suggest starting with her local genealogy librarian. If she hits a dead end, maybe hire a genealogy geneticist. I tell her I hope she finds her father.

As the emails continue, so does my struggle with my racial identity.

Standing before numerous audiences, uncertain of who I am racially, like an uncomfortable mantra, I keep repeating, "I'm a white woman with Black heritage," looking out at the sea of mostly white faces, sometimes interspersed with people of color.

And every time I do, I believe it less and less.

CHAPTER 5

The Whitest Black Man

AFTER A YEAR OF GIVING BOOK TALKS AND PUBLIC LECTURES ON RACE, being consistently asked after each presentation how I identify racially, I still cling to the answer I gave on *The Megyn Kelly Today Show*:

I'm a white woman with Black heritage.

But I can't shake the Black woman's condemnation on Amazon that I'm betraying my Black ancestry.

Adding another layer to this question of racial identity, a mixed-race man who saw the show contacted me with his family's converse racial secret. His family hid their white ancestry.

Although his family secret is white heritage and mine is my Black heritage, I realize that both of our families' need to hide a part of their mixed-race identity is rooted in other people's prejudices and racial expectations. My mother's words chime in my head: *How will I hold my head up with my friends?*

Intensifying my confusion and uncertainty about my racial identity is a frank discussion of racial identity that occurs after I give a presentation on *White Like Her* at a Chicago suburban library. The enthusiastic audience is a blend of white and Black people, many eager to share their thoughts on racial identity.

A Black woman, who identifies herself as African American, relates her husband's story. She jokingly refers to him as the whitest Black man she's ever seen. Her husband, she says, attended an all-Black high school and college and both his parents are Black.

Before they were married, his parents made a startling confession. They told him he was adopted. Just as startling, they revealed that his birth parents are white and from England. It was a grandparent from Argentina who gave him his slightly brown hue.

Even after learning that his birth parents were white, he said he still considered himself Black. His reasons were: He was raised by Black parents, felt connected to the Black community, went to Black schools, and had a Black wife.

However, the woman adds that he felt "funny" (her word) about finding out, which is understandable. His sense of who he is has been destroyed—a huge identity shift. Not only are his parents not his birth parents, but genetically he's white.

In deciding to continue identifying as a Black man, for him, culture and life experience supersede his genetics. By claiming a Black identity, he defied not only genetics and his appearance but also the idea of race, becoming an outlier who deviated from ingrained notions of race. He also shined a light on race as a social construct and the arbitrariness of racial identity.

Like him, in my identifying as a white woman with Black heritage, I was choosing the culture I was raised in, not my mixed-race genetics. But unlike him, whose appearance belies his chosen identity, my physical appearance matches my white identity. For the majority of my life, no one ever questioned my racial identity. I look white. End of story. If I hadn't written a book about my mother's passing as white and been thrust into the public arena, no one would ever question my white identity.

So, how do we determine our racial identity in relationship to our genetics? Should our DNA be the deciding factor? There's no easy answer.

Northwestern University's Center for Diversity and Democracy (CSDD), in conjunction with 23andMe, explored that complicated question in a national survey in 2018. The study assessed people's perceptions and attitudes toward race and genetics. The study found that "a majority of Americans agree that someone's racial identity is not hard-wired into their DNA . . . 51 percent think race is separate from biology, while only 34 percent said that they believe biology 'totally' determines racial identity."[8]

However, there were significant differences between subgroups.

"Individuals who identify as white were significantly more likely to think that information contained in their DNA is a factor determining racial identity. Indeed, 66 percent of whites—versus 53 percent of Asian Americans, 52 percent of African Americans, and 51 percent of Latino Americans—believed that their racial identity is 'determined by information in their DNA.'"[9]

What interests me about the study's conclusions are the factors the participants thought determined racial identity.

When looking at what factors make up race, almost half (48 percent) of the participants thought that skin color was the best way to determine racial identity. A close second are culture and family history.

"Thirty-five percent believe[d] that culture plays an important role. . . . About an equal number of respondents, 34 percent, see family history as the most important factor determining a person's race. Finally, 18 percent . . . believed that race is determined by an individual's 'personal choices' about their identity."[10]

It's important to note that the CSDD clearly defines race as a social construct, which I agree with in theory. However, in the real world—the everyday world of racism and bigotry—race as a social construct seldom figures into how people view race. And putting people into racial categories is often used as a way to justify social inequalities.

To explore the findings of his study, Professor Alvin Tillery Jr., director of the CSDD, did his own experiment with his Northwestern University class. He showed his students "a genomic pie chart of someone who is 26 percent Scottish/Irish/U.K. and 74 percent West/Central Africa." He told the class that the genomic scan belonged to someone in the class. Unbeknownst to the students, the chart was Professor Tillery's. When he asked them whose genomic chart it was, most students thought it was someone who could pass for white.[11] Looking at the professor's photograph, it's evident that he couldn't pass for white.

So where does that leave mixed-race people like me? Do we adhere to the racial identity that is determined by our skin color and appearance? Or do we choose another factor to racially identify ourselves, such as culture and life experience, as the whitest Black man did?

In continuing to identify as white with Black heritage, appearance and culture play into my answer, as does my desire to be sensitive to African Americans who've endured discrimination and worse because of their skin color.

As the African American woman in St. Louis, who was a member of the Black caucus, said to me when I identified as a white woman with Black ancestry: "Any other answer would have been wrong."

If family history is also a determining factor of racial identity (34 percent), what about my Black and mixed-race ancestors? How do I factor into my identity their long history of racial discrimination and trauma—from my fifth great-grandmother Marta, an eighteenth-century enslaved woman who bore her enslaver thirteen children, to my mother's oppression under Jim Crow laws? Although I hadn't directly felt the sting and suffering, they certainly had.

Considering all the factors of racial identity from skin color, to culture, to family history, I'm still not comfortable declaring myself anything other than white with Black heritage. In a few short months, clarity will come from an unexpected source.

*Parts of this chapter first appeared in an article I wrote for *The Washington Post, Inspired Life*, "I thought I was white until I learned my mother's secret. The census helped me tell my family story."

CHAPTER 6

A Racial Identity I Can Live With

WHEN YOU'RE SEARCHING FOR AN ANSWER, A WAY TO BE YOURSELF IN THE world, when your identity has been shattered and you don't even recognize yourself in the mirror, the answer sometimes appears when you least expect it.

Professor Lori Tharps asked me to be a guest on her podcast, "My American Melting Pot," to talk about *White Like Her* and my mother. I have a hard and fast rule: If at all possible, I accept all legitimate invitations to talk about my story. Professor Tharps explained that I'd be sharing the podcast, "The One-Drop Rule Revisited," with Philadelphia-based journalist and writer, Shannon Wink. Shannon learned that her maternal grandfather wasn't Native American, as he'd claimed. He was Black.

My mother's great grandmother, Mary Brown, made the same claim to explain her darker skin tones. She even named the tribe—Cherokee. There was a nameless, eighteenth century, Native American female ancestor in my family tree, but it was on the paternal side.

During the podcast, skillfully guided by Professor Tharps, Shannon and I discuss our racial family secrets and what it means to be white or Black in this country. *How does knowing we have Black ancestry change our sense of racial identity? What role do culture and community play in our identities?*

All the questions I've been struggling with for years.

Professor Tharps points out that if the one-drop rule was still the determinant of one's Blackness, both Shannon and I would be designated Black. But, of course, we're too white-looking to be considered Black.

Then she brings up an incident from one of my appearances that she'd watched.

She said that she chuckled when I explained to the white host the paper bag test for mixed-race people.

During Jim Crow, if your skin was the color of a brown paper bag or lighter, you were allowed to join certain organizations, fraternities, and sororities. In New Orleans, where my mother grew up, there were "paper bag parties." You had to be a certain complexion to attend them.

"In a sense, Gail, you're a racial ambassador, explaining Blackness to white people, opening up a dialogue where they can talk to you about Blackness. You're an in-between person. How do you feel about that?" Professor Tharps asks.

The idea of being a racial ambassador never entered my mind when I wrote the book, or when I did my presentations.

"I never thought of it that way. But in a way, I guess that's what I am," I answer.

I don't know if I'd call it an *a-ha* moment, but something clicked for me. Suddenly all the pieces of my racial identity came together.

Although I was uneasy in the role of racial ambassador, Professor Tharps was right: My mother's story has given me a public platform to talk about race. It has also given people permission to question my racial identity, and in turn, possibly their own.

This constant questioning made me dig deeper, go under the surface of my white skin, to delve into what it means to one's identity to have mixed-race and Black ancestry. In the blend of white culture and multi-racial family history, I finally understand who I am. Considering my DNA (7–9 percent African, 2 percent Native American), my ancestor's history of subjugation, my mother's choice to pass as white, and my public platform, I decide that mixed-race is the identity that best defines me.

I realize that some people may feel I have no right to claim a mixed-race identity, but I believe I have an obligation to do so. Standing before an audience, so blatantly white, and declaring myself mixed race, I challenge people to think differently about race.

My choice of a mixed-race identity is my truth; not the truth of how others—whether Black or white or mixed race—see me, or how they think I should identify based on their own racial beliefs.

Choosing "Other"

I no longer check "Caucasian" on medical forms. I check "Other." If there isn't a box for "Other," I make one. "Don't think you know me," is my silent message. I'm not what you perceive. If a doctor should ask me about my racial choice—and none have so far—I'll happily explain my rich racial ancestry.

When I filled out the 2020 U.S. Census form, I selected multiracial for the first time, stepping out of the shadow of my mother's racial secret. I like to think she'd be pleased with my choice, or at least pleased I can make that choice. It's a different time, a different era.

When the results of the 2020 U.S. Census were made public, I found out that I wasn't alone in my choice. In the 2010 census, some nine million identified as mixed race, but in the 2020 census, that number rose to 33.8 million—a jump of 276 percent.

If I hadn't gone public with my Black heritage, I probably wouldn't have joined the fastest growing racial and ethnic population in the United States.

While my choice of a mixed-race identity goes far beyond the color of my skin, I realized that my whiteness protects me. Even considering the increased numbers of multiracial Americans, I'm not unaware that racism and bigotry still gnaw at this country. If telling my mother's story can at least make people think about the damage racism causes, then I've nudged the needle.

Sometimes I believe it does. So, I keep telling my mother's story.

After one of my talks at a suburban genealogy society, a white woman approached me.

"I was so moved by what your mother went through, I had to speak to you," she says. "I used to work with a man who was an affirmative action hire. I resented him every day. I wanted to tell you that I'm so ashamed. I'll never feel that way again."

As I told Professor Tharps when she asked me if I had an agenda in writing *White Like Her*: "I'm not a politician or a crusader, I'm a storyteller."

The power of story, in listening to other people's lives and struggles, allows us to open ourselves to empathy and understanding. In the brave telling of our stories, we heal ourselves and others.

*Parts of this chapter first appeared in an article I wrote for *The Washington Post*, *Inspired Life*, "I thought I was White until I learned my mother's secret. The census helped me tell my family story," by Gail Lukasik, October 13, 2021.

CHAPTER 7

The Salmon King's Daughter

Kara Rubinstein Deyerin: Maple Valley, Washington

KARA USED TO CARRY A PHOTO OF HER BLACK FATHER TO PROVE WHO SHE WAS.

"No matter where I went, I never looked right. When I told people I was biracial, I wasn't believed. Even when I showed them my dad's photo, I could see they didn't believe me."

* * *

Kara's home office seamlessly blends her family and professional life—files neatly stacked on an expansive desk, behind which hangs a child's drawing—his name printed in large black letters; a green leafed plant shares a window sill with a framed blue imprint of a child's hand.

"I'm always cautious with my journey, especially with issues of race," Kara states. "So, before we begin this interview, I want to make sure that my beliefs and perceptions are not misconstrued or misrepresented."

As the CEO and founder of Right to Know, I understand her

caution—how exposed she must feel on a daily basis, dealing with issues of unexpected racial and parental discoveries. But as I quickly learn, that's not the only reason she's hesitant.

"We've realized over the years that the media wants the sensational side," Kara continues. "We insist if you're going to use our 'crazy' stories, and they are 'crazy' stories, please list resources for help. Because when someone has a surprise, they're devasted."

I relax and reassure her that I'm happy to put a list of resources at the back of the book, thinking how lost I was when I discovered my mother's racial secret and how such a list would have been extremely helpful. But then I bore the weight of secrecy.

"Okay," she says hesitantly, still leery of my intentions.

Then she begins her story with a murder.

*　　*　　*

"My story is intertwined with the murder of my mother's parents when I was four," explains Kara. "They were murdered in international waters off the coast of Tahiti. The FBI was involved. We think her stepbrother murdered them. Though it was never solved. Obviously, it impacted my mother and me."

She has a calmness, probably hard won, as she tells me about the murders and how her mother never felt safe and had to keep moving in fear of her stepbrother. Every so often a sadness flickers in her dark eyes quickly replaced with a smile.

She blames the murder for her early transient life of poverty, growing up in the projects in a white neighborhood on the East Side of Seattle.

I think how some lives are determined by tragedy nearly impossible to endure or overcome. And how, sometimes, these tragedies blossom into careless decisions that eddy out like a stone thrown in a still pond.

I wait a beat to see if Kara will reveal more about her grandparents' murder. She does.

"My mom was twenty-three when her parents were murdered. She was a single parent. My father wasn't in the picture by then. They divorced when I was one year old. You see, he was a heroin addict. That's how my parents met, in a rehab place. He was there for heroin addiction. My mom's parents put her there, because they caught her smoking marijuana. It was a place for hardcore drug addiction. That's where they fell in love."

Being placed in rehab for smoking marijuana seems like an overreaction, possibly revealing her grandparents' strictness and her mother's rebellion against it. Kara believes her mother marrying her father was part of that rebellion. I understand her impulse to protect and explain her mother's actions.

Wanting to steer the conversation toward her racial identity, the essence of her story, I ask how her race is listed on her birth certificate. She just happens to have her birth certificate handy because of homeschooling one of her sons during the pandemic.

"It's not listed. I don't think race is listed on birth certificates."

I tell how my mother was designated "col" (colored) on her birth certificate—one of several documents that proved my mother was passing as white. Kara thinks it's because my mother was born in the south.

"And in 1921," I add.

"Anyway," she says offhandedly. "If you grew up with two people in your household, you just assume they're your parents. My dad was Black and my mom white. I assumed I was biracial."

Racism's Many Shades

"Oreo," "half-caf," "mutt"—those are some of the names Kara was called growing up. In fifth grade, a girl asked her if she was mixed. When Kara said yes, the girl slapped Kara across the face. Yet, even in those instances, Kara didn't want to pass, ignoring the advice of her beloved Black grandfather, Pop, who'd experienced the violence of racism.

"If you need to pass, you should," he advised her.

"I wouldn't ever want to do that," she told him.

"No baby, you don't understand," he stressed to her. "If times turn to how they used to be and you see me on the street, you have to pretend you don't know me and walk on by. You have to pretend we're not related."

"My olive skin allowed me, if I wanted to, to travel the world as white," Kara says. "But I couldn't understand why someone would want to pass. I wanted to embrace all of who I was."

As hurtful as those instances of racism from outsiders were, the racism within her own family seemed especially cruel and confusing.

"My first memory of my father's parents was when I went to stay with them for a week. I was seven. My grandmother hated me because I was so white-looking. . . . It was a terrifying experience."

The bluntness of her statement surprises me. Kara explains that her grandmother's hatred for her stemmed from her mother divorcing her son. But she's quick to add that her grandmother didn't like white people—because she almost died because of racism.

Her grandmother's story of near death reflects the many shades of racism in this country. Arriving in Seattle from Oklahoma in the middle of a snowstorm, the only place open for her to seek shelter was a "white's only" bus station. Forced to wait outside in the storm, she was freezing and hypothermia was setting in. Then a white police officer spotted her and invited her to sit in his car.

Kara laughs at the irony of her grandmother's story.

"So, I never quite got it. Whatever her hatred of me was about, she treated me differently. Skin color is a big issue in the Black community. My grandmother was very dark with a red undertone. In that household, I was light, and they were dark."

It's difficult to understand her grandmother's disdain for her seven-year-old, mixed-race granddaughter that extended to taking all her grandchildren school shopping except Kara.

It was her grandfather, Pop, who offered her protection. She told him that she hadn't been treated to school clothes. He must have chided his wife because the next day her grandmother took her shopping.

"She bought me a turquoise blue skirt and a striped red and turquoise sweater. I remember it. She never did it again."

That one moment of acceptance forever lodged in Kara's memory. Despite her grandmother's rejection, her grandfather and other family members did accept her.

To Kara, fitting in with her Black family meant that when she was with them, she adopted their vernacular.

"I got really good at code-switching. If you didn't see me, I sounded like everyone else in my Black grandparents' house. But when I went home to my mom, I had to switch. Because I'd get in trouble if I wasn't speaking properly."

I'm reminded of my mother purging herself of her New Orleans accent as a way of assimilating into her white, middle-class lifestyle in Ohio. She permanently code-switched.

Kara stops, considering her next comment about her mother's white family.

"It's not that I felt that my mom's family were racists. But they're white and I'm not. I'd hear them say, 'She's got that Black dad.' I was different there, too. And I felt that my entire life."

She was so invested in her Black identity; she challenged an elementary school secretary who wanted to change her race on a school questionnaire.

"When we moved to Seattle, my mom marked me as Black on a school form so I could have access to the gifted programs for minorities. At the time, you could only choose one race. The school secretary summoned me to her office. She took one look at me and said, 'I'm changing your race from Black to white.'"

"You better not," Kara responded defiantly. "My uncle (Kara's father's brother), is the president of the Seattle school board. You might have to answer to him."

"She left me Black," Kara states. "I didn't understand the concept of the program. I thought I was having to fight for who I was. And I was proud of my African heritage. So, of course, I'm going to fight for that." She pauses. "I've had to prove my identity all my life."

The Big Reveal

"I wanted to go to Africa and find out where I was from. When you're Black in America, you don't know what that means. I said to my dad, 'C'mon, Dad, don't you want to know where in Africa you're from? So, I got these DNA kits from a Thanksgiving Black Friday sale. I gave him his for Christmas. I did mine first."

She sets the scene, taking me with her into that momentous instance that shattered her sense of self. And although I know what's coming, I need to hear it in her own words, to see if it echoes my own experience of lost identity.

"I'm in bed. It's morning. I'm checking my email. I see the message from 23andMe and click on it. I'm half. My pie chart is half."

She stops, takes in a deep breath.

"Then I read my ethnic makeup. I have zero African DNA. *Zero*. The half is Ashkenazi Jew. My mom's not Jewish. And my dad certainly isn't Jewish. It was like a punch in the gut. It was like those movies where the camera goes spinning off."

Her first reaction? It's a mistake. They switched vials.

"My kids and husband are in another room watching TV. At that moment, it's all about me. I went into a private room, called a friend who worked on mapping the human genome."

Her friend told her to open up her maternal matches and see if she recognizes any matches. She did.

"You know what that means, don't you?" her friend said.

Kara laughs.

"I did know what that meant. I'm not Black. That's my whole identity. That's what I grew up with. That's what I fought for."

Her friend told her she could be whoever she wanted to be. But for Kara it wasn't that simple. In a split second, the foundation of her life crumbled.

"What you believe from that sacred relationship with your parents is gone. You're not you."

It takes Kara a few days to reach her mother, who was vacationing in Arizona. When she told her mother about her discovery, her mother said, "DNA doesn't lie."

"I was grateful. Because I now know that most moms when confronted say the DNA is lying. Then, I asked her, 'Who is it? Who is my father?'"

"'I have no idea,' my mother said."

"Were you angry with her?" I ask, baffled by her mother's response.

"No. Shocked, bewildered, and confused. I spent four months in a fog. You can't look in the mirror. I can't stress that enough for people who haven't had this happen to them. You want to hang towels over every mirror in the house. In the bathroom I'd almost crawl under the mirror, so I wouldn't have to look at myself. It's not you. You don't see you. It's a stranger. You have no context for this person looking back at you. Most people have that reaction. But sometimes people stare in the mirror. 'Who is that person?'"

Kara leans toward the computer screen as if to demonstrate this unsettling experience.

"It's either: I can't look at all, or I can't step away from the mirror trying to figure out what I'm looking at."

"You know what my dad said to me when I told him? He said, 'You swapped one oppressed people for another.'"

She chuckles, then adds, "I'm the only white person I ever met who grew up thinking they were Black."

* * *

Later, I'll reflect on how she suffered for her Black identity: the slap in the face, the racial slurs that stung and imprinted, how she defended her Black identity as a child to the school secretary, how proud she was of her Black culture. All gone in an instant.

What goes into that space, that half that is no longer her? I wonder.

Then, I think how fortunate I was that my mother's "lost" family found me and embraced me. That my appearance on PBS's *Genealogy Roadshow* led them to me. Not for the first time, I realize the extraordinary circumstances of that occurrence, which was not the case for Kara.

Who the Hell Am I?

"I sprayed the internet with my DNA," Kara jokes. "I wanted to know from day one who my biological father was. Who the hell am I? You can't begin to heal until you know."

Kara went on every single data base: Heritage, 23andMe, Ancestry, GED, and DNA Painter. Finally, after a year, she found a match, a second cousin once removed who never answered her email inquiries.

But she persisted, eventually piecing together her family tree. It was then she saw the photograph of the man she believed was her father based on his age, his physical resemblance to her, and her shared centimorgans.

Centimorgans are units of genetic measurement. Experts use this information to help describe how much DNA you share with your relative. The amount of centimorgans you share with somebody determines how closely related you are.

"Oh, my god, I'm totally related to him," she says, capturing that moment. "The resemblance was remarkable."

It was a transitional moment for Kara, seeing someone who looks like her. For her whole life, she felt like she didn't fit in because she didn't look like anyone in her family. Suddenly, she saw her own face in this man.

What Kara describes is genetic mirroring, a crucial element in constructing our identities and our connection with family. We bond with family partly because we look like our family. Being able to see ourselves in family members provides us with cultural, racial, and ethnic roots.

When she reached out to the man who she thought was her father, he was ill with memory issues. He told her to talk to Ava. When she asked him who Ava was, he said, "I don't remember." (Ava is a pseudonym Kara uses when discussing her story.)

Although the man couldn't remember who Ava was, he did give Kara her contact information, which eventually led to Kara finding her. Their meeting would be a turning point in her search for her biological father, upending her belief founded on her genetic research that Sam Rubinstein, affectionately known as "The Salmon King of Seattle," was her grandfather.

"As I walked up Ava's sidewalk, she came up to me and grabbed my arms crying. 'You look just like Sam. Your eyes are identical. You have that twinkle.'"

She smiles at the memory. "Which was so funny, because I've been told my whole life that I have a twinkle in my eye."

When she said to Ava that her eyes were like Sam's because he was her grandfather, Ava's response stunned her.

'No,' she said, 'I think he's your father.'"

Although Ava seemed convinced of Kara's paternity, Kara wanted to be sure. She asked if she would do a DNA test. Ava agreed. Based on Kara's and Ava's DNA match as second cousins, another close family match, and some more distant matches, she was able to triangulate these matches to show that the man she thought was her father was her half-brother.

And that Sam was her biological father.

Well-known and highly successful, Sam Rubinstein was a prominent businessman and philanthropist, who took his father's cannery business and turned it into a major salmon canning company. In addition to his business acumen, Sam was an ardent supporter of the arts in Seattle, serving on the boards of the Seattle Symphony, the Seattle

Opera, the Seattle Art Museum, and the Seattle Chamber Music Society, among other arts organizations.

But her delight in finding her birth father was bittersweet. Sam died in 2007. And upon learning that Kara was Sam's biological daughter, the family rejected her.

"Money was their first thought. The fact that my father's family is so wealthy really complicated things. I can't even get information about the family's medical history. Because I'm a mother, I feel that they're rejecting my children, too."

She hesitates before continuing. "Sometimes I wish he was the electrician down the street. But on the flip side, there are like five hundred articles about him. And because he donated so much money to the arts, there are a lot of pictures of him as well."

"And your mother?" I ask her. "When you told her about Sam Rubinstein, what did she say?"

"When I knew who my birth father was, I said, 'Mom, how did you meet this Jewish guy?'"

"In a bar," her mother answered sheepishly. "I honestly didn't think he was the father. I thought you were two months early. I thought your dad was your dad."

Kara questioned her mother's belief.

"'Mom, if I'd been two months early, my lungs wouldn't have been developed. I would have been kept in the hospital.' But she kept insisting I was a miracle. That when her husband who'd left her came back for his stuff, they had sex. She believed in her mind that's when I was conceived. It was a truth she told herself for so long, it became her truth."

As any daughter would, Kara wants to protect her mom. I understand the impulse. I felt the same way about my mom when my book came out and people criticized her for passing, seeing her as a race traitor.

"My mom feels guilty because she saddled me with a father who wasn't there for me. I think that's why it's taken her a year to finally admit what really happened. I've forgiven her, but I don't think she's forgiven herself."

Fighting for Her Jewish Identity

Wanting to fully embrace her new paternal identity, Kara decided to change her father's name on her birth certificate to Samuel Rubinstein. Not an easy feat, especially when the birth father's family is rich and powerful.

To that end, she engaged a family law attorney.

"All I wanted was acknowledgment," she explains. "I had to hire a genetic genealogist because I needed her statement to try and change my birth certificate. I wanted to be as sure as I could be that Sam was my father. In Washington state you have to essentially file a paternity suit to change your legal parentage. Also, to change my birth certificate, I needed a respondent. The problem was Sam is deceased (and so are the executors of his estate), as well as his son. So, I had no one to name on the document."

Kara and the Rubinstein family finally ended up settling with a nondisclosure agreement. Kara agreed to give up all her claims/rights and her children's rights to any inheritance. In exchange, she is free to talk about her story.

"That was the most important thing for me. Being able to talk about my discovery and that Sam's my father.

"You can't heal until you have an identity." Kara says. "I just wish you could convey that 99.9 percent of the time when people make these discoveries and are reaching out to the family, they just want connection. They just want to know who they are. What makes them tick. And if there's any medical issues they should be concerned about. The last thing on anybody's mind is money."

"It's hard, though, because I have to color this discovery with growing up fighting for my Black identity. And now, I'm having to fight for my Jewish identity."

Kara no longer carries a photo of her Black father. Instead, above her computer screen she keeps three photos—Sam Rubinstein, her mother, and herself.

The resemblance between Kara and Sam Rubinstein is striking—same twinkle in their eyes, similar smiles, similar hair.

She touches the computer as she explains why.

"It helps me, seeing the people who gave me life. How I came to be. It's a crazy reality. I've only had this reality for a short time. I have to look up and say, 'That is who I am.' It's my way of coping, I guess."

CHAPTER 8

A Tale of Two Sisters

Jane: New Orleans, Louisiana

FOR JANE, HER RACIAL IDENTITY WAS NEVER IN DOUBT. IF PEOPLE THOUGHT she was Hispanic or white, that was their problem. She knew who she was—Black. But for Jane's sister, her racial identity was in doubt. Eventually, it became a matter of life and death for her.

Jane contacts me via Facebook Messenger. Her opening statement stops me in my tracks.

This is my sister who decided one day with her husband to be white.

Below her message is a blurry colored photograph of two women dressed in shorts and sleeveless tops sitting side by side on a bench with three children. They share the same generous smile and warm olive skin tone. A heart emoji clings to the right-hand corner of the photo.

The abruptness of her opening sentence and the accompanying photograph pull me in like all compelling stories do. I'm hooked.

There's a breathlessness to the rest of Jane's message. As if only the visual will keep me reading, she intersperses family photographs of her mother and father, and of her and her sister, who both could easily pass for white.

Finally, Jane tells me why she contacted me.

"No one ever writes books about the effects of passing on the family members who lost their love ones to be another race. . . . Once someone passes, it's like a death to the family." A crying emoji punctuates her loss.

The next text box says, "One day she was here and the next day they were all gone. Would you write a book on how passing affects the family? . . . I would gladly tell you the entire story."

I've spent the last several years talking about my mother's story of passing—what she lost, what she gained; about racism and its ugly history in America from slavery to institutionalized racism; but I've never explored it from the point of view of the people left behind.

Intrigued, I decide to contact Jane and set up a Zoom meeting. I want to hear her entire story.

Most People Leave Town, But She Didn't

"One day my sister decided to be white," Jane states. Her flat tone masks the hurt in her eyes.

I study her black wavy hair, the warm olive tone of her skin, her full lips, and her large red framed glasses that magnify her dark eyes, so reminiscent of my mother's. She could be kin. But she's not. Still, I can't shake that feeling of familiarity.

Does she feel it, too? I wonder.

The day her sister decided to be white was Christmas 1975. Jane had spent the day wrapping presents for her sister's four children and her parents. Jane's two daughters were excited to see their cousins and grandparents. A close-knit family, they spent weekends, holidays, and birthdays together. The photographs she sent me seem to support their closeness.

Jane explains that they were running late that Christmas, so she called her sister and told her they were on their way.

"No, you can't come over," her sister said.

"Why can't I come?" Jane asked, perplexed.

"Well," her sister hesitated. "My husband has people from his job over. He doesn't want you here."

"What do you mean?" Jane felt a clutch in her stomach.

"They're white. And you know."

The "you know" hung in the air between the two sisters.

"And I'm not white. Is that what this is about?"

Jane stops her story and looks down. When she raises her head, I see the anguish etched on her face, an anguish she's carried close to fifty years.

"After that, I never saw her again until my mother was dying. She didn't talk to me anymore. She didn't see me anymore. The children didn't see each other anymore." She takes in a shuddered breath. "And they didn't leave town. They were right here. Only twenty minutes away. Most people leave town, but she didn't. They just stopped talking to everybody."

Her face goes soft with confusion.

"At first, I was angry, mainly for my mother. She was no longer allowed in my sister's house. She knew about the birthday parties and the graduations, because they still talked. But she couldn't go. It hurt her. But she never complained."

As if I'm not understanding the gravity of what her sister did to her and their family, Jane adds, "Listen, my sister wanted to pass so badly that when she became white, she made my mother take all her pictures out of her house—wedding pictures, graduation pictures, baby pictures all disappeared. I have no pictures of my sister when she was young, because she took them when she left."

What baffles me is the suddenness of her sister's decision. And the timing. Was there something else behind her sister's decision to pass? Something Jane didn't know?

When my mother permanently passed, it was 1944. Jim Crow laws still ruled the south. But when Jane's sister passed in 1975, the civil rights movement of the 1960s had transformed the racial landscape. In 1964 and 1965 the federal government passed historic civil rights legislation, formally banning race discrimination in voting, employment, and public accommodations. And the Racial Discrimination Act, which prohibited discrimination on the basis of a person's race, was passed in 1975.

So why pass for white in 1975?

Leslie Alexander and Michelle Alexander point out in their essay, "Fear," that these gains were largely symbolic to Black people, "who were subject to pervasive police violence and trapped in segregated impoverished ghettos that had been created by white racism and government action."[12]

Regardless of these changes on the federal level, in Louisiana in 1975, race was still determined by the one drop rule. It wasn't until 1983 that Louisiana used a less stringent mathematical formula for designating race. If you were one-third African descent, you were Black. Louisiana was the only state to use a mathematical formula.

Even today, with the one-drop rule a relic of the past, David Wright Falade keenly observes in his *New Yorker* article, "Mixeded," that to white society "mixed race" means "Black."[13]

How Could You Leave Your Family?

According to Jane, there are understandable ways and reasons to pass. Wanting me to understand her sister had other choices than leaving the family, Jane tells me about her father, an enigmatic man who even in the faded photographs looks Italian, with his trimmed mustache, sharp nose, and slightly wavy hair. He's in contrast to his darker-skinned wife, who Jane refers to as "brown," meaning "brown-skinned."

"Back in the day, you had to work as white to get a decent job. Daddy looked white, so he worked as white."

Jane is referring to the Jim Crow south era, a period of legalized racial segregation and discrimination predominant in the Southern United States, which lasted from the late nineteenth century to the mid-twentieth century. During that time period, people of color were relegated to low-paying menial jobs, such as factory workers or housekeepers.

Jane continues, "I understand that. But I don't understand leaving your family to be with a bunch of strangers. If they found out what you were. Why would you want to be with those people?"

What Jane tells me next goes to the heart of racial identity for mixed-race people and the dilemma of passing. But for Jane, it's about family loyalty.

"But when my father came home, he was Creole or whatever you want to call it. He didn't bring the white people to his house like my sister did. He didn't associate with them outside of his job. That's what most people who worked as white did. But when they came home, they became who they were."

Although her father retained his Creole identity at home, his identity wasn't fixed. He dwelled in two different worlds—only one reflected his authentic self. The other identity he assumed was based on how others saw him. Daily, he had to decide which world to inhabit and when, then act accordingly.

But it went beyond work when Jane and her parents were in public places.

"When I was a kid, one weekend my dad took me to St. Louis Cathedral and the French Quarter. My mom didn't come with us. I'm sure my mom didn't want to raise any questions about what she was. He had me passing and I didn't even know it."

I ask Jane if she ever passed.

"I never had a desire to pass. To me, passing is too hard."

"Do you identify as Black?" I ask, wanting to understand how she sees herself and not how others see her.

"I'm New Orleans Creole." You can hear the pride in her voice.

Then she launches into her definition of Creole and outlines the criteria by which a person is considered Creole, and I start to feel uncomfortable, as if I'm listening in on a conversation I have no right to hear.

"In the Creole community, you were designated by your hair and your color. And it was called 'good' hair. Or 'bad hair,'" Jane explains. "The way it worked was if you were brown, you had to have good hair to be Creole. If you were light, you could have bad hair. To be Creole, you had to have one or two or both. The Creole people thought in three races: the white, the Black, and the Creole."

My feelings of unease increase.

Then to my relief, she adds, "It's not like that anymore. Thank God. But I identify myself as New Orleans Creole. But if you asked me my race, I'd say Black."

What She Did Was a Betrayal of the Family

Jane circles back to her sister, the reason she contacted me and what still haunts her.

"What my sister did was a betrayal of the family. How could she leave her family?"

Without rancor, she says, "I know your mother did the same. And I can't understand that either."

I try to explain the difference—that my mother, unlike her sister, kept in contact with her mother and siblings. But the truth remains. My mother hid her racial secret from my father, my brother, and me. And only those family members who could pass as white were allowed to visit us.

"Here's the crazy part: Her husband left her with six kids to marry a *real* white woman," Jane continues. "My thing is, when he left, why didn't she come back to the family? She didn't work. She didn't need to pass. I was told she couldn't come home because her children were raised as white."

After her husband left her, it was a downward spiral into poverty for Jane's sister. Her electricity was turned off and she was too frightened to claim child support because she was afraid the courts would see the different races of her children. Yet, she stubbornly refused to return to the family.

The last time Jane saw her sister was at the hospital when their mother was dying.

"At the very end of my mother's life, I saw my sister once at the hospital and I told her off." She laughs nervously and looks down, clearly distressed. "I shouldn't have done that. But I told her off. I said to her, 'You know, you shouldn't have done what you did. That's wrong. You know, being white is not better than being Black. You shouldn't have been ashamed of who you are. And giving up your family.'"

"What did she say to you?" I ask, understanding how grief overtakes you.

"Nothing." She shakes her head with regret.

"When my mom finally passed away, my sister sat by my mom's bed in the hospital and looked at her. I guess she was crying. Then she just left and didn't say anything. Afterwards she came to the church with two of her children, went to the graveyard, and then they went home. I never saw her again. I mean it's so sad."

"What happened to your sister?" I need to know how the story ends.

"She died. I wasn't even told. My cousin called me from Texas and asked if I'd seen the paper. When I said no, she told me to sit down. Then she told me my sister had died.

"They didn't put any of our names in the paper. They didn't use her maiden name. It just said mother of six children, grandmother of three. Nothing about us. Loving daughter of, you know. The obituary was in the paper two weeks after she was buried. They made sure we couldn't go to the funeral."

"What are you feeling toward your sister now?" I ask.

"I wish we could do it all over again. I wish I could tell her.

Sometimes I feel bad that I never talked to her and tried to find out why she wouldn't come back to us, to the family, when her husband left her."

Even through the computer screen her sadness is palpable.

"How different it would be if she had not passed as white. She had six children. None of them talk to me, except her oldest grandson. My brother and two of his kids are dead. His other kid is estranged from the family. I have my two daughters, my grandchildren, and my great nephew from my sister's family. That's it. You asked me how I feel. It's terrible."

* * *

In the months that follow, as I listen, record, and transcribe other family secrets, I think about Jane and her sister—the stark loneliness of Jane's life; the betrayal and abandonment that destroyed her family; how only family can inflict such deep, lacerating wounds. I also think about her sister's children, who will never know their true racial heritage, unless one day on a whim they take a DNA test. Then what they thought they knew about their racial identity will be forever altered. Will they go in search of the family members lost to racial passing?

Once again, I'll debate the wisdom of publicly sharing one more family secret of my own, weighing the possible hurt I might cause against the good I could do. All the while probing, incising others' secrets in the service of understanding what family is.

As Margaret Atwood said so aptly, "All writing is motivated deep down by a desire to make the risky trip to the underworld and to bring someone or something back from the dead."

Do I have the courage to make that journey again? To delve into the last remaining piece of my family's racial story: What did my brother know?

CHAPTER 9

___

Straddling a Racial Divide
Bruce-Paul Scott: Mt. Vernon, Washington

GROWING UP IN A WHITE IRISH CATHOLIC FAMILY OF TEN CHILDREN, BRUCE-Paul Scott knew something was different about him. His dark curly hair, easily tanned skin, and dark brown eyes didn't mesh with his nine fair-skinned, blue-eyed siblings.

When he finally learned the truth of his racial identity, both his parents were dead, and he was left with an unthinkable dilemma about his conception. There were only two ways he could have been conceived. Neither one bore thinking about.

*   *   *

Kara Rubinstein Deyerin, CEO of Right to Know, suggests that I interview Bruce-Paul Scott.

"We both live in the Seattle area and have become friends. Our stories are in direct contrast to each other."

While I wait for her to introduce us via email, I read Bruce's narrative on the Right to Know website. His story is succinct, lauding the DNAngels who helped him find his biological father. DNAngels is a non-profit organization that assists people in identifying their biological parent or parents.

Even more enigmatic than his narrative is his small black-and-white photo, which tells me nothing definitive about his race and ethnicity.

When I see Bruce on the Zoom call, I'm hard pressed to put him in a racial box. Sixty-nine years old, he sports a shaved head and a salt-and-pepper mustache. There's an easiness about him and a hard-won vulnerability I sense under the surface.

I tell him he doesn't look biracial.

"I shave my head. I didn't like people asking me where my curly hair came from. It's a total conflict every day. Every big damn day."

He offers to send me photos from his youth.

In the photos, he does look biracial, especially the photo of him as a young man, possibly from the early seventies, sporting an afro hair style.

Where'd You Come From?

The first eleven years of Bruce's life, his burgeoning family moved ten times, because of his father's work as the international representative for the United Auto Workers union.

Living in white neighborhoods and attending white schools, Bruce could count on two things: rude questions about his appearance and his parents' insistence he was white.

Even before his family settled in Tulsa, Oklahoma, as young as four, children asked, "Where'd you come from?" Often followed by "Where'd you get that hair?" Questions he had no answer for.

His dad told him, "Tell them your hair came with your head."

The clever punchline did little to quell Bruce's anxiety about how different he looked from his white schoolmates. Only inside the warm and supportive cocoon of his tight-knit family did he feel accepted.

"It was when I went outside the house and someone would taunt or bully me that I felt profoundly different," Bruce says.

When his father threatened to send him and his siblings "back to the Indians" for misbehaving, Bruce thought maybe he was adopted or Native American.

Then, in sixth grade, the taunts turned malicious.

When I ask him what the kids said to him, he takes a sip from his coffee before answering.

"Have you ever been called a nigger?"

The shock of his answer stings. I say no.

"I was called that. And 'half-breed,' 'Brillo pad,' 'little black sambo.' I didn't even read that book. Then there was this teacher, Mrs. Johnston."

Before he relates the story, he stresses that he was a good student, with a good singing voice and not disruptive, confirming that his being ostracized was about his dubious racial appearance.

His class was chosen to participate in a city-wide sing-along held in downtown Tulsa.

"Although I was in the choir, I was the only one who didn't go. When I asked Mrs. Johnston why, she said that I didn't sing well enough. There were five thousand kids singing at different times. I'd been in choir the entire year and I wasn't ready? I was the only one who looked like I did at that school. It was very clear to me that I wasn't welcome to go there."

However, the discriminatory racial incident that really seared him occurred in 1965, when he was fourteen.

"I went to this church service with this girl. We weren't dating. I was dressed very well." He qualifies the situation, letting me know that it could only be his looks once again that prompted the church lady's censure.

"This white woman came up to me after the service and said, 'Young man, I want you to know we do not approve of these types of dating situations in our church.'"

Naïvely, at first, he thought it was because he was Catholic.

"But I wasn't wearing Catholic clothes or something."

He looks away as if he could escape the painful memory.

"When I got home and thought about it, I realized that the way I looked was going to affect my dating life. And it did. Throughout my dating time, even after I got back out of the service, I now recognize that as soon as I met the parents, the relationship would cool. . . . It reminded me of the 'guess who's coming to dinner' situation."

"Did you ever talk to your parents about the discrimination you suffered—the hateful bullying, Mrs. Johnston, the woman at the church?" I ask.

"When I did say something, they would give me a lukewarm nonresponse. They were never going to tell me the truth. They'd give me some line of bullshit about recessive genes.

"There was this one time when I was thirteen. My dad was driving me someplace at night. We were alone and I was talking to him about my situation. It was one of the very few pieces of advice he gave me. He said that someday I would see my situation, the way I looked, as an advantage. I didn't understand it at thirteen. I was just trying to dick my way through school. My thought was: *How is this going to be an advantage?*"

Left in the silence of his parents' unwillingness to address his physical differences, he struggled with his racial identity. His parents kept telling him he was white. The outside world kept telling him he wasn't.

When I inquire about his birth certificate, he laughs.

"Listen, you couldn't write better fiction than my birth certificate. It says I'm white. That my father is Charles Scott. I was born on September 22, 1952. The date is scratched through. September 21 put in its place." He smiles. "Yeah, my birth certificate says I'm a white guy."

Then in 1972, Bruce was drafted into the Army and once again his appearance impacted his life, putting him in a life-and-death situation.

Undercover Work

During the Vietnam War, Bruce was stationed in Germany. After a year serving as an MP (military police), the army decided his skills were best suited to investigating crimes. For his last and most dangerous assignment, he worked undercover as a drug investigator.

"My cover was a biracial school teacher working for the department of the army or defense. They picked me because I was an ambiguous-looking person who talked really well."

Working in conjunction with the German police, his assignment was to buy two kilos of heroin at a specified apartment. It was a buy-bust. The plan was he would be arrested along with the drug dealers. But something went wrong.

"I'm sitting there in the apartment with these drug guys, five thousand Deutsche marks in my hand, hash on the table, and no gun, waiting for the police to come. Only problem, the police go to the wrong apartment," he laughs, making light of what must have been a harrowing experience.

"The intelligence got screwed up. The drug guys hear this commotion, and suddenly there were more people in the room than I'd at first seen. One of them has a gun. By this time the police bust in, the element of surprise is missing. One guy tries to go out the window. And there I am with no gun. I thought, *this is screwed.*"

Bruce pauses. "I think about it daily."

The irony of being asked to "play" the part of a biracial school teacher fed into his continuing doubt and uncertainty about his racial identity, reenforcing his suspicion that his parents, who refused to acknowledge his differences, were hiding a secret about his parentage.

In 1974, when his parents visited him in Germany, Bruce remembers the wonderful bittersweet visit.

"It would have been the perfect time to tell me. But they said nothing," he says.

And he'd stopped asking, knowing he'd get the same answer. "You're the product of a stray recessive gene. And your father is your father."

Even when his mother was dying, she said nothing. After her death, he hoped that she left a letter with an attorney, explaining everything.

There was no letter.

He was stranded in the limbo of his racial identity.

Although he dated after he left the army, his uncertain racial heritage impacted his relationships with women. One woman, who he was engaged to, couldn't handle the fact that he didn't know his lineage and what her future with him and with their children would be. She broke off the engagement.

He didn't marry until he was forty-seven-years-old. And he never had children.

"In my darkest moments," Bruce says, "I think one of the reasons I don't have children was 'how would I ever explain this to somebody?'"

Beyond a Reasonable Doubt

In 2014, Bruce took a commercial DNA test to settle his ethnicity.

"When I spat in the tube, I told myself I'd follow the leads wherever they went."

Where they went didn't surprise him. What the outside world had been telling him since he was a child was true. He was biracial—37 percent of his DNA was Saharan African. But he needed more information if he was going to make sense of who he was. Did any of his siblings have African heritage?

Using his training as an investigator, he methodically built a DNA profile comparing his DNA with two of his siblings through commercial DNA tests. His oldest sister had zero African DNA. With his youngest brother, he did a XY chromosome test. (XY chromosomes are commonly known as the sex chromosomes. Males inherit an X chromosome from their mother and a Y sex chromosome from their father.) The test indicated that he and his brother didn't share the same father.[14]

"To eliminate the fact that I could have been switched at birth, I did another mitochondrial test with my sister," Bruce explains.

This test was to determine if they came from the same mother. They did. The conclusion based on the various DNA tests: he and his siblings had the same mother, but he had a different father.

"What was that moment like, when you found out your father wasn't your father?" I ask, knowing he might not want to revisit that moment of family betrayal.

Before answering, Bruce gets up and refills his coffee cup, taking a moment to gather his thoughts. When he returns, he looks intently into the screen, making sure I understand.

"Suddenly it all made sense to me."

If his father wasn't his father, who was? And what had been the circumstance of his conception?

With little to go on, Bruce was stymied.

Then a Black woman found him on Ancestry, giving him his first lead. Based on ancestry's DNA match, she was Bruce's third cousin on his father's side. Was she the key to understanding his nebulous genetics?

His third cousin lived in Arlington, a mere seven miles from Grand Prairie, Texas, where Bruce was born. Excited at the prospect of meeting a paternal relative and possibly discovering who his biological father was, Bruce flew to Arlington to meet his cousin. However, she proved reluctant to share with him any information about the people she knew who were related to him.

Although discouraged, he wasn't going to give up in his quest to find his biological father. His breakthrough came when he discovered the organization MPE Friends Fellowship and met Laura Olmsted, founder and Executive Director of DNAngels, a lifeline for MPEs seeking their biological family—"*Finding Families, one DNA strand at a time.*"

As stated on their website: "In an effort to promote family

connections, we support, guide, and assist adults searching to accurately identify their biological family through analyzing DNA results."

Under their mission statement, in bold letters, is the statement: "Many DNA discoveries can bring up hidden trauma," followed by a list of resources.

Thanks to Laura and DNAngels, Bruce finally learned the identity of his biological father. He emphasizes that he was Laura's first client and possibly the longest. During the six-year search for his birth father, Laura never gave up, persistently and aggressively following every lead.

"She was just a bull dog, a damn bull dog. I found out his name in January 2021."

When I ask if he wants to share his birth father's name, he hesitates. Then, in a determined voice, he tells me his name.

"You're the first person that I told his name to."

I thank him for his trust.

"Yeah, well, I didn't have a concept of him then. I do now. It's not really a good one. I don't have a 'I'm glad he gave me life.' Screw that. Somebody else would have or I'd been a turtle."

From Laura, he also learned that his father's family line goes back to the 1700s in America and that his second great grandmother was enslaved.

"I'm descended from slaves," Bruce says.

Then his tone changes and his sentences become clipped as he describes his biological father.

"I found out he was an uneducated laborer, construction guy, probably traveled around doing labor jobs. Raised on a farm in east Texas. Born 1907 or 1913. Died as a young man. He was less than sixty. He only had a third or fourth grade education."

The description offers no clue as to how his mother, a white woman with three children at the time of Bruce's conception, became involved with a Black laborer. In 1950s east Texas, an interracial sexual relationship was a crime. If caught, his birth father could have been lynched.

Not Your Cousin, but Your Brother

Left with too many questions, several years passed without resolution. It wasn't until May 2021 that Bruce had another breakthrough. A Black woman who'd found him on Ancestry emailed him, also believing she was his third cousin.

When Bruce checked their connection on Ancestry, he received a shock. They shared 1700 centimorgans. The exact same number of centimorgans that he shared with his white sister. Centimorgans don't lie. The Black woman wasn't his cousin; she was his biological half-sister.

As Peter Boni explains in his book, *Uprooted*, "a centimorgan is a measurement of how likely a segment of DNA is to recombine from one generation to the next. . . . When two people have a DNA match, it means they inherited DNA from one or more recent common ancestors. The length of the DNA they have in common is estimated in centimorgans. The higher the number, the closer the relationship."[15]

Because the woman and Bruce shared 1700 centimorgans, they would be classified as "Close Family" (1450 to 2050 centimorgans). In this category the relationships are grandparent to grandchild, aunt or uncle to niece or nephew, or half-sibling.

Bruce explained to the woman, whose name was Rosa, that they weren't cousins, but half-siblings. That he was her half-brother.

The news was so upsetting to the woman, she began to cry.

"You mean my dad's not my dad?"

Although their biological father had been hidden from Rosa and Bruce, because Rosa's mother was Black, her race was never in doubt.

After several phone calls, Rosa finally understood that her mother had had a relationship with Bruce's birth father and that they were siblings. Like Bruce, she'd been born in East Texas in an area her family was from.

In addition to Rosa, Bruce also discovered he had a niece. His niece and her husband had known his biological father.

When Bruce questioned them about his birth father, they described him in his youth as a gambler and a drinker who maybe ran around a lot, sowing his wild oats. But when he married and had a family, he turned his life around and became ultra-religious.

But what still troubled Bruce: What were the circumstances of his conception?

Whatever they were, his parents had protected him and his mother's secret by passing him off as someone he wasn't—his white father's son.

Georgina Lawton, author of *Raceless: In Search of Family, Identity, and the Truth About Where I Belong,* who also had a Black father and white mother and was passed off as white by her parents, explains the difference between passing and being passed off and how it harms a child's identity. Unlike passing, where a person knowingly pretends to be something they're not (as my mother did by passing as white), in being passed off, the person isn't aware of the deception. In both cases, a part of the person passing or being passed off is sacrificed.[16]

"If you are being passed off, such as children unwittingly being raised by fathers who aren't their own, it brings the deception to a whole new level. Being passed off requires a 'passer' (a parent) to make the choice for the 'passee' (the child). . . . Being passed off requires participation from a range of others to uphold the story and this can inflict a whole heap of psychological confusion on the passee, whose world is warped as others play pretend too. The passee's interaction with others will be disfigured, as they will all be asked to suspend belief and sustain false realities."

The parents passing off the child usually are hiding a shameful secret and in doing so believe they are protecting the child from societal scorn, as well as themselves. But what they fail to take into account is the loss of intimacy and trust that occurs when the passee discovers they'd been lied to and betrayed.

Bruce still struggles with why his parents didn't tell him the truth once he became an adult, leaving him to speculate. There are only two scenarios he can imagine and neither one gives him comfort.

A Traumatic Event

"I'm 99 percent sure my mother was raped." He touches his heart when he says this, emphasizing the fervor of his belief. "It's nothing I can prove. Yet."

He relates how other NPEs (those conceived through a non-paternal event) he's talked to, in an effort to make him feel better, question why he would think one way or the other about his conception, because of a lack of proof.

"I just shut them down," he says. "I knew my parents. For one thing, when I was conceived my dad wasn't gone from home for long periods for his work. And if there was a problem in their marriage and my mother was looking for fulfillment outside the marriage, why in hell would she pick a Black man who was an uneducated laborer to have an affair with?"

His explanation is difficult to hear, weighted in shame and fear and uncertainty. But he tries to understand their decision to remain silent.

"The event of my conception was so traumatizing to my parents' relationship and marriage it was just going to be something that they swallowed, buried, and moved on with."

Then he adds, "Maybe I feel more comfortable that it was rape, than to accept the fact that my mother might have been unfaithful. It's really my decision that I get to make. From listening to other NPE's stories, I know that no matter what happened, to live with this secret you have to protect your parents to continue to love them."

When I ask him if he was angry with his mother for not telling him, he shakes his head.

"I felt sad for her. What a wasted opportunity for me to be able to show compassion for her. To understand what had occurred."

His words hit home. My mother's continued silence, even after I confronted her with the truth of her racial secret, was a wasted opportunity for intimacy, and I felt nothing but sadness for her.

He takes a deep breath.

"People ask me, 'Did your dad know?' He may not have known if she'd had an affair or been raped, but he damn sure would have known when I was born, and he saw me."

Sister Rosa

Between our first and second interview, Bruce flies to California to meet his sister Rosa. When they first meet at Rosa's apartment, he tells me, she cried. He calls her a sweetheart. He uses the same word to describe the sisters he grew up with, showing his total acceptance of his biological sibling.

And, as it happens with so many meetings between "lost" family members, Bruce stares at Rosa, trying to see resemblances in their physical appearance. The need for tribal connection is so strong.

"Among the oddest things was just looking at her," he explains. "It was like seeing me for the first time in my life. Though we had different mothers, we have similar eyes, doe eyes."

Not only do they share physical similarities, they both worked in graphic design: Rosa as a typesetter and Bruce as a graphic designer. Another common bond.

He considers her his sister, not half-sister. Just as he considers the siblings he grew up with as sisters and brothers, not half-siblings, even though they don't share the same father.

Straddling a Racial Divide

Although Bruce now knows he's biracial, he feels that the psychic, psychological, and identity issues will go on forever for him.

"I accept the fact that I'm biracial, but I don't think I'll ever be totally comfortable. I still have to work it out in my own life. And the only way I think I can do that is to be an example for someone else," he pauses. "It would be my guess that you don't have another person you interviewed like me. I'm always looking for someone who has a similar story to mine. It could be a Black man who was raised in a white family or a white guy in a Black family. Never found one."

As the interview winds down, I ask if it's okay to use his real name.

"You can use my real name. There's not going to be anyone who'd be offended or defended. I want to help other men. I want people to know I am out here. My dad said that someday what I was going through would be an advantage. This is the advantage time."

CHAPTER 10

The Black Sheep of the Family
Josephine, PsyD, LMFT: Napa, California

JOSEPHINE HAS THE DUBIOUS DISTINCTION OF NOT ONE, BUT TWO PARENTAL discoveries—one at age twelve, and the other as an adult.

As she expresses her feelings about these discoveries, she holds up one finger and says, "The first one was welcomed." Then she holds up a second finger. "The second was unwanted. That's my story in a nutshell."

Josephine, a psychotherapist with a doctorate in psychology, tells me she was drawn to her profession because she saw it as a way to make meaningful changes in society.

True to that altruistic impulse, when she had her second discovery, she decided to specialize in parental discovery, leading her to pioneer the only mental health treatment protocol dedicated to DNA surprises, called *Parental Identity Discovery*. She's also written articles for *Psychology Today* on subjects, such as family secrets, trauma, coping with unexpected DNA test results, and identity.

"When I had my 2014 DNA discovery, I found I was trying to teach my therapist why I needed help, why this would be a trauma. It's so easily dismissed by a large number of clinicians. The confusion seems to lie around the impact of identity."

She lists some of the dismissive statements made to people coping with misattributed parentage experiences (MPE), which I've also heard from other MPEs.

You know you're really no different. You're still the same person. You're still part of our family.

Your dad is still your dad. What's the problem here? Does that change who your dad is?

Her expertise on the impact of a discovery on identity is one of the reasons for my interview. The other, of course, is her fascinating story of her two misattributed parentage experiences.

Life or Death Secrets

Josephine's openness invites confidences—a trait that must serve her well as a psychotherapist. Sitting in her home office, I can only see a sliver of the space—a pulled shade, corner of a fireplace, and a bookcase displaying pottery. On the top shelf is a framed picture of a blue butterfly—an apropos symbol of her own transformative journey, changing identities not once, not twice, but three times.

Before we begin, I say, "Maybe it's just me. But I believe these stories need to be heard."

She shakes her head, meaning it's not just me.

"These stories need to be heard," she reiterates.

* * *

For the first twelve years of Josephine's life, she believed that her mother's second husband, Steve, was her father. But it was a troubled marriage.

"I think he was mostly her ticket to get outside of her very small western Pennsylvania town," Then she adds, "I don't know how much love there was to begin with. But that's not for me to say."

When they married, the Vietnam War was raging. As a major in the army, Steve served two tours of duty in Vietnam. When he returned, he was traumatized, probably suffering from PTSD. He turned to alcohol for relief, and he and Josephine's mother began to drift apart.

After the war, part of Steve's military obligation required him to be gone three weeks every month, which only added to their marital problems. Left alone in California, far away from family and unhappy in her marriage, her mother began a series of affairs. Although Josephine can't prove it, she believes that there was an understanding between Steve and her mother concerning her affairs. She describes her mother's sexual behavior as trying to make the most of a bad situation.

Pregnancy didn't appear to be an issue because her mother had had her tubes tied several years earlier in an Army hospital. But the sterilization didn't work. She became pregnant with Josephine.

Because there had been several affairs happening at the same time, her mother wasn't sure who the father was. What she did was choose the guy she thought was the dad, Wade (soon to be Josephine's stepfather), and worked out some kind of understanding with him. They would pretend that Josephine was her husband's child in order to not upset the balance of her family life.

Josephine now realizes that her paternity was a secret to everybody except her real biological parent.

"Even the man who supposedly was my father, my stepfather Wade, didn't know. I find that astonishing."

Rather than condemn her mother's duplicitous behavior and secrecy, Josephine explains it within the cultural context prevalent during the thirties, forties, fifties, and maybe even in the sixties. Josephine compares her mother's hiding the identity of her biological father to my mother's decision to pass as white during a time when revealing her true racial identity might threaten her life.

"I've come to view my mom's secrecy somewhat as a life-and-death response. Not that she'd be killed like in Jim Crow south, but another kind of death, being cut off from family. My mom is still living in that social conditioning," Josephine says.

From a twenty-first century perspective, it may be difficult for us to understand why Josephine's mother might have viewed her situation as one of life or death; one that she still can't escape, keeping her locked in her own secrecy of shame.

Today, women who have multiple sex partners or live with their sexual partners aren't labeled "sluts" or "whores," or viewed as sexual deviants. If they have a child without the benefit of marriage, the child isn't necessarily labeled a "bastard." Often, unmarried women refer to their child's father as their fiancé, suggesting marriage is in the offing, even if it isn't.

From my own experiences growing up in the 1950s and 1960s, the religious and societal pressures put on women regarding their sexuality were hard and fast. If a woman strayed outside these religious and societal strictures, she was shamed and, in some cases, shunned by her family. On the other hand, men were afforded the freedom to explore their sexuality without the fear of being ostracized and scorned.

I have a very vivid and disturbing memory of a "sex" talk given to my eighth-grade class. The girls were herded into one room; the boys into a separate room. Each talk was delivered by a priest.

The gist of the girls' talk was that we would have sexual urges that we were more capable of resisting than the boys were. The boys, being boys, couldn't help themselves and easily lost control. Because our sex drive was weaker, it was our moral duty to say no, to repel the boys' advances.

The priest actually said, "You are occasions of sin." He might as well have handed out chastity belts at the end of his misogynistic lecture.

At such a young, impressionable age, under the iron fist of the Catholic church, it was a difficult message to totally ignore. The religious censure was reinforced by family and society. If a girl became pregnant out of wedlock, as Ann Fessler so poignantly chronicles in her book, *The Girls Who Went Away*, she was sent away and her child surrendered, or she was married off. It was never talked about again, or never talked about at all. But the shame remained. As Josephine says, another kind of death.

Josephine explains that MPE moms still view their sexual secret as dangerous. They're still frozen in that strict culture they grew up in, which perpetuates their shame and silence. And the sad part is that these moms can't forgive themselves. They still believe their families will cut them off if their secrets are revealed.

It's not hard to understand why Josephine's mother kept the truth of her paternity secret. And it's not hard to understand the trauma for the MPE that's caused by the secret—leaving a painful divide between the MPE moms and their children. For the MPEs, however, not knowing the truth of your identity, who you really are, is just as dangerous and life threatening.

A Different Dad

A couple of years after Josephine's birth, her mother left Steve, mainly because he was an abusive alcoholic. After that, Josephine had weekly Saturday visits with him, unaware that he wasn't her father.

When Josephine was four years old, her mother married Wade. In Josephine's opinion, Wade was a much better choice than Steve—the father who was listed on her birth certificate.

Eight years later, her mother finally decided to come clean. (At least in her mother's version of coming clean.)

"How would you feel about Steve not being your dad?" her mother asked.

"Actually, that would be great," Josephine answered. To her, Steve was horrible. Losing him as her birth father was no great loss.

Then her mother dropped a bombshell.

"Your stepfather, Wade, is your dad."

"Great," Josephine said.

Josephine explains her response.

"My stepdad had been there from my earliest memory. He was a dad in every possible way. Probably aren't many better than him."

To legally prove that Steve was not Josephine's biological father, he had to submit to a DNA test.

As Josephine's mother must have already known (or at least suspected), the DNA test proved Steve was not Josephine's father.

I ask Josephine if the test also proved that Wade was her biological father.

"My parents were only trying to prove that Steve wasn't my father. The legal counsel wasn't interested in proving who my father was. In hindsight, I suspect that maybe because everyone knew Wade wasn't my father was why he wasn't tested. This was substantiated by a conversation I had with their attorney a few years ago when I was researching who knew the truth of my paternity."

Once it was established that Josephine wasn't Steve's daughter, Wade formally adopted her. Her last name was changed, and she officially became a part of Wade's family.

"I never saw Steve again," Josephine says.

At the time, she didn't fully comprehend how destabilizing it had been for her, losing a father, even an abusive one, to another father, and having to shift from an English heritage to a Jewish one.

"It was a tremendous loss. That I didn't understand. Now I know that I was experiencing grief, trauma, and identity confusion. What I call a tripod experience. And unlike when a parent dies and there's an outpouring of support from the community, and an acceptance of your grief, often an MPE discovery isn't viewed in the same way." Josephine pauses. "You really can't fully understand this loss unless you've experienced it."

Although her stepfather was now her biological father, Josephine felt something wasn't right. The family were never warm toward her.

She credits the family's aloofness in part to their natural personality styles and dynamics as a family, and the rest to suspicion.

"My grandmother never believed I was her son's child," she explains.

And she just didn't look like anyone on Wade's side of the family. Yet, still as a child, she searched for a connection with his family—now her family.

"I'd look at them and say how am I related to them if I don't look like them? I'm the only redhead on either side of the family. There's only one other relative with blue eyes. I would look at my grandmother's thumbs and I would say, 'okay, I have the same shaped fingernails. Yeah, yeah. We're related.'"

But in the end, none of it was real.

The Story I Didn't Expect

In 2014, Josephine decided to take a DNA test.

"It was my way to try and learn more about my history and my dad. His side of the family was never forthcoming or inclusive with me about anything."

Josephine's reaction to her family's not sharing their history with her reminds me of my own mother's reluctance to share her New Orleans family story, the absence of pictures of her father, her claim she didn't know when he was born, or when he died, which prompted my search for my elusive grandfather, Azemar Frederic. Such absences inspire a seething curiosity that isn't easily extinguished.

Josephine believes that MPEs know intuitively that there's a family secret concerning them, but don't know what it is.

The 2014 DNA results showed Josephine was 50 percent Scottish and Irish on her father's side and about 41 percent Italian on her mother's side, with no percentage of Ashkenazi Jewish heritage. It took her two years to fully comprehend the implications of the results.

When I ask her why it took her two years to understand the implications, she says it was "probably a self-protective mechanism at play." Possibly the emotional blow of losing another father was too much for her, as well as the revelation that her mother lied to her again about her paternity.

Lacking the emotional bandwidth of taking on the arduous task of finding her biological father, she hired a genealogical investigator. Although the genealogist found her biological father in two weeks, she waited to tell Josephine. She couldn't find a residential address confirming that he was in Moraine County in 1973. Apparently, he was off the grid. Eventually, the genealogist located a real estate license that placed him in Moraine County in 1973.

After two false positives, Josephine now knew who her biological father was. But his identity left too many unanswered questions. She needed to meet him, to look into his eyes, hear his voice, and have him explain why he was never a part of her life.

The genealogist coached Josephine on how to make contact—through a registered letter, as well as a voice message. To Josephine's disappointment, he sent the registered letter back and left her voice messages unanswered.

Realizing she wasn't going to get any information from him, she made the bold decision to go to his house, which isn't generally recommended.

"I needed closure. I wasn't going to be able to sit with nothing," Josephine explains.

Her voice quickens with excitement as she relates her first encounter with her biological father.

"It was Labor Day weekend 2017, Sunday morning. I knocked on his door at nine a.m. When he opened the door, I told him who I was looking for."

"'He doesn't live here,' he replied."

Josephine takes a deep breath, as if she's standing on her father's doorstep, seeing him for the first time, hearing him deny who he is.

"I was not prepared for that response," she says.

While his denial threw her, the more concerning piece for Josephine was the way he was looking at her.

"There was a kind of longingness in his eyes—a softness to his face that you just don't have when you're trying to send someone away from your doorstep. His body language didn't match his behavior. I was able to recognize that because of my training as a therapist."

Not knowing what else to do, she left. Josephine and her husband pulled over down the street and just sat in the car unsure what to do. Her husband asked her if she wanted to leave.

"I kept going back to his face. Who looks at someone that way if they don't know them? He knew who I was," Josephine states. "I look a lot like my mom. I figured he must be recognizing her in me. So, I went back."

Josephine's not sure why he opened the door to her, but before he said anything, she shoved her phone in his face. On the screen was his high school yearbook photo—the only photo that the genealogist was able to find.

"'I think this is you. And you're my dad,'" she told him. "'I think you know my mom. I just want information.' He was very quiet and shocked as anyone would be. But he invited us in."

Three hours later, Josephine left with an entirely different story than the one she expected. Finally, she had some pieces of the puzzle. Though not all.

She smiles as she relates what she learned from her biological father, John.

"He knew about me from conception. He was one of the affairs. At the time, he was living with my mom as a renter. That's why we couldn't find a residential listing for him. He was the real estate agent who sold her the house. He was with me for the first two years of my life, taking care of me, knowing that I was his. When he no longer felt welcome, he left. In his words, he 'saw the handwriting on the wall.'"

I ask the obvious question: "Why didn't your mother tell you who your biological father was?"

"I still don't know. I think when she considered John vs. Wade," Josephine gestures with each hand, "that Wade was the better choice as a parent. And she was right. John is a nice man, but he's not cut out to be a dad. And he knew it. He has a son eight years my senior who he had an on-again, off-again relationship with. My mother picked the right one. I ended up having the right kind of life."

"And my mom swears up and down that the whole time she thought I was Wade's." Josephine grimaces with skepticism. "I have doubts about that. And that has created some problems between us."

Lost Time

As in so many of these stories of hidden parentage discovered, there's the bittersweet element of lost time. Josephine had four and a half years with John. He passed away in 2022.

During those four and a half years, Josephine was finally able to piece together the scattered pieces of her identity.

Josephine calls the experience surreal. I imagine her sitting in John's living room, taking notes, studying him, no longer so desperate to belong that she has to find similar thumbs, as she did with her supposed grandmother.

From John she learned her ancestors were adventurous people who journeyed from Scotland to Canada, finally settling in the United States. She knows the highland town her people came from, what ship they took to Canada, where they homesteaded. She knows things any daughter would know, such as what college he attended.

And over time, Josephine didn't feel as lost. The holes left by the loss of her Jewish, German, and Russian identity were filled with her father's Scottish heritage.

"Suddenly, I started to feel like I was standing on my own two legs again. I had a sense of who I was," she explains.

Josephine believes that the MPEs who adjust better to these

discoveries are the ones who gain information, even if it's just a name. With that name, they can get a sense of their cultural and ethnic background.

Yet, the ones who have the best chance of integrating their new identities are the ones who actually meet their parent(s) and/or family members. From them, they can obtain medical information and more personal family history, as Josephine was able to do after meeting her birth father, John. And they can finally see themselves mirrored in their birth families—a profound and centering experience.

In explaining why it's so vital to MPEs to find their birth parent or parents, Josephine leans toward evolutionary psychology. She believes MPEs are seeking their primal deep-rooted self that comes from DNA, which goes counter to the nurture theory.

"Though we live in the twenty-first century, that limbic part of our brain, our oldest mammalian part of our brain is still functioning in a tribal way. That still registers that if you're not identified as part of our tribe, then you're against us," Josephine states.

"Ironically, this limbic part of the brain is also what convinced MPE moms that they needed to keep their secret at all costs. For some MPE moms, they're willing to attack their grown children for broaching the subject at all. They will cut them off, declaring, 'How dare you do this to me? It's my life.'"

Many of these moms will go to great lengths to protect their secret. They view it as a threat because they still fear being ostracized from their families.

As Josephine points out, "If you're not part of your tribe, you're in the out group. From an evolutionary standpoint, this is a dangerous place to be. When you're alone and not part of a tribe, your survival is at risk. It's a matter of life or death."

The Cost of Breaking the Silence

No longer willing to perpetuate the silence of her mother's secret, Josephine went public with her story: on her professional website, in her articles for *Psychology Today*, and in her podcast, where she and a genealogical investigator narrate interviews with real people who've experienced shocking non-paternal events.

Breaking the secrecy came at a cost.

"I ended up being the black sheep of the family. I'm a reminder of a shameful act that places me outside the family, outside the tribe. For Wade's family, I began as a stepchild, then suddenly I'm a biological child, and now I'm back to stepchild again. They just don't understand it to this day. The fact that I went searching for John, my biological father, found him, and then went public with it became a terminal obstacle for us. We no longer speak."

Her relationship with her mother didn't fare much better. Josephine describes it as practically nonexistent.

As our interview winds down, she shares a recent personal experience that goes to the heart of why it's important for MPEs to find and possibly connect with their biological family in order to heal.

"My dad, John, died quite suddenly in January. We went back to Tucson where he was living and where his sister, my aunt, lives. My half-brother and I scattered his ashes. We have an extremely close relationship, my half-brother and I."

She touches her heart as she tells me this.

"As an only child, having a sibling is probably the best thing next to having my own kids. I sat with my aunt, my brother, two first cousins, and I just kept feeling like a sponge. 'Tell me more,' I kept saying. 'I just want to be around you.' I felt more complete that day than I've felt my entire life. And it keeps getting better and better as I keep adjusting to my 'new' self, my 'new' identity."

CHAPTER 11

My Two Dads
Terry: Abilene, TX

TWO YEARS AFTER LEARNING THE TRUTH OF HIS PATERNITY, TERRY'S STORY made the news on a local TV station in Abilene, Texas.

An intriguing human-interest piece, it had all the elements of a made-for-TV movie—a handsome protagonist in search of an unknown father, a family's hidden secret, and a happy reunion.

Wanting to approach Terry's story with fresh eyes, untainted by another journalist's take, I resist watching the newsclip until after I write Terry's narrative. As expected, there was nothing new in the TV clip, except the photographs. The most striking are the senior high school photos of Terry and his biological father, placed side-by-side for comparison.

Terry explains during our interview that when he saw the two photos, "It was game over."

What this two-minute TV appearance doesn't reveal is what lies below the eye-catching headline and the fairy tale ending—a person still struggling to integrate who he thought he was with who he now is.

It's easy to like Terry. His warmth, charm, and positivity radiate through the computer screen, overcoming his work office's utilitarian background. A self-described IT nerd, he sits in front of four monitors, wearing headphones. In college he studied the saxophone with two renowned classical saxophonists. But, he says, it was technology that won his heart.

Throughout the interview he crosses and uncrosses his arms, leans back in his chair, not that he's uncomfortable telling his story, but because he's bursting with energy and emotion.

Latino-Rooted

Terry's life was built around his Latino identity. A militantly proud Latino, he not only learned Castilian Spanish, to his Mexican grandmother's delight, but he married a Spanish woman.

In his Mexican American family, Terry's nickname was *Guero*. Since it's a common Mexican-Spanish word to describe someone who is light-skinned, he never thought anything of it. There are many light-skinned Mexicans who have a higher degree of European ancestry. And his mother was a blend of European ancestry—German, Polish, Scottish, and Irish.

To him, his immersion in Mexican culture seemed a natural expression of his Latino pride and led to his very public Latino persona as one of the founders of a social media company that tells stories of Latino voices not covered by major networks. It's still in existence today. As a very public Latino, Terry accumulated over twelve thousand Twitter followers.

Was he trying to prove that he belonged in his tightknit Mexican American family that boasted sixteen grandchildren? Or was it his overriding belief in justice and fairness for everyone, including Mexican Americans, that impelled him to embrace his Latino identity? Or both?

"I always wanted to be someone who cared about the rights of others," Terry says, recalling the racism his parents endured. "When they were living in Arlington, Texas, in the late 1960s, they woke one morning to a burning cross in their front yard. You know dark skin and white skin."

Knowing what he knows now about his genetic heritage, he admits there were hints. He just wasn't tuned into them.

Why would he be? Certain things you shouldn't have to question.

As Maya Angelou said so eloquently, "The ache for home lives in all of us, the safe place where we can go as we are and not be questioned" (*All God's Children Need Traveling Shoes*).

I would add, "and not be deceived."

It's Time to Tell the Truth

What led to Terry's shocking discovery was a family medical concern.

"It was our son's health that propelled us to turn to 23andMe. We were looking for genetic mutations to help us treat certain social and emotional issues he was experiencing," Terry explains.

Though the DNA test confirmed that there were genetic mutations on Terry's paternal side, it also indicated that he had no Spanish or Mexican ancestry. His paternal side was 40 percent Ashkenazi Jewish.

His first thought was that it was a mistake—a common reaction of many MPEs.

"I was laughing about it when I called my mom. I said jokingly, 'I really think I am the mailman's kid.' At the time, I didn't realize she was hemming and hawing."

Near the end of the call, his mom told him that his maternal grandmother had been adopted, continuing the deception.

After they hung up, his mother called a close cousin and asked her what she should do. The cousin told her that it was time to tell the truth. She texted Terry.

"I need to talk to you face to face."

"As soon as I got that text, I think I knew. I was at work. For the rest of the day, I was absolute garbage. I felt very out of body. I call it emotional paralysis. On the twenty-minute drive from my office to my mom's, I felt like I was floating."

His mom was waiting for him in her backyard. When she saw him, she broke down crying. She admitted to making some mistakes when her husband of six months was in Vietnam. Taking advantage of her uncontrolled freedom, she dabbled in drugs, alcohol, and had multiple sexual relationships.

Then she said, "Your dad is not your biological father."

"That's when I just lost it," he says.

At first, he told her he didn't want to know who his biological father was. In his mind, his dad was his dad. But by the end of the conversation, he asked who he was.

She didn't know.

Although Terry admits that at the time he was angry and hurt with his mother and father for withholding the truth of his paternity, he now talks about his mother's behavior with love and understanding.

"My mom was seventeen, married, her husband is in Vietnam, and she's kind of going crazy. Doing what she never got to do. We're talking about the early seventies, the late sixties. It's a free time, living in the wake of Woodstock. Living in the age of nuclear proliferation. My perception of that time was people were living in the moment."

It was also a time when abortion was illegal. While access to birth control pills was legal for married women in 1960, it was prescribed for "purposes of family planning, and not all pharmacies stocked it. Some of those opposed said oral contraceptives were immoral, promoted prostitution, and were tantamount to abortion."[17]

Terry believes that if his mother wanted to, she could have had a back-alley abortion. But she never considered it.

In his narrative on the Right to Know website, he comments on society's double standard at the time.

"I . . . feel that society will often celebrate a man's sexual exploits and then turn around and shame a woman for behaving the same way."

When his father returned from Vietnam, his mother met him at the airport. It was obvious she was pregnant. He asked for some time apart. About three days later, he came back to his wife and said, "This isn't the way I was planning to do this. But you're my wife. We're going to raise the child as our own and never talk about this."

Terry admires his father for raising another man's child, but he disagrees with their decision not to tell him when he was older, especially considering that the family knew.

"My grandparents knew the whole time that I was the dirty secret. Nobody ever told me. That's shocking to me."

It Was Game Over for Me

For the next three to four months, it was a real struggle for Terry just to get out of bed each day and go to work.

"I went from Mexican to Ashkenazi Jewish. My two sisters were now my half-siblings. My dad wasn't my dad," Terry states.

"I felt like I'd been a fraud my whole life. I felt like I'd been deceived."

Wanting to help him, his mother gave him a name of someone she had a relationship with while her husband was in Vietnam. His DNA wasn't a match, nor was the second person's, whom she personally called.

After the second failed attempt, he told her he needed to take a break.

Eventually, he decided to try Ancestry, thinking he might find a first or second cousin. After six agonizingly long weeks, his results came.

Anxious, he skipped the ancestry section and went directly to the DNA Relatives page. At the top was a first initial and last name. He and this person shared 3,425 centimorgans across seventy-six segments.

The analysis of the genetic possibilities of their connection indicated that this person could only be his father.

Excited, his heart thundering in his chest, he took the man's first initial and his last name, which was unique, and cross-referenced them on Facebook and Classmates.com. He discovered a match.

When he looked at the person's senior class photograph, he knew he'd found his biological father. They had the same facial structure, eyes, and features. Plus, he'd graduated from a high school in the same district as Terry's high school.

"It was game over for me. This is him. I mean it's the same face. And that was bizarre. I'd never experienced that before."

Terry was experiencing genetic mirroring.

Before contacting his biological father, he reached out to his dad and asked his permission.

"You're my dad," he told him. "You're never not going to be my dad until the day you die."

In what can only be described as a loving and generous response, his dad told him he deserved to know this, and that he'd had the honor and privilege of being with him and watching him grow.

His next step was to seek advice from the online MPE support group, he'd been participating in. One of the members suggested he use a template letter. Rather than wait, he decided to write the letter the same day. It didn't take him long to find his biological father's full name, address, and phone number.

In his letter, he included the genetic strip from Ancestry that showed the centimorgans they shared. He gave information about his mom, such as where he might have met her. He made it clear that he was a self-made man, happily married with a beautiful family, and didn't need anything from him. He just wanted to know his new family history. At the end of the letter, he said, "If you were open to it, I'd like to buy you lunch or coffee." He included his and his biological father's senior class photos, as well as a photo of him, his wife, and two children.

Then he mailed the letter. Three days later, he received a text message from his biological father. In the text, he said that he was surprised to receive his letter, that he'd be very happy to put together his family history for him, and that he was open to having lunch or coffee.

Terry called him the next day.

During their forty-five-minute conversation, which Terry describes as warm and friendly, he learned that he had three half-siblings, all of whom are engineers. Even more surprising, his biological father was a retired project manager, the same position Terry currently holds at a large bank.

His biological father had no idea he existed. Terry's conception had been the result of a one-time encounter.

The following week, Terry and his biological father met for lunch. During the three-and-a-half-hour lunch, Terry learned about his grandfather who suffered from mental illness and committed suicide in his fifties, confirming another piece of his medical history.

After learning of his grandfather's suicide, Terry wondered if his grandfather had met him, would it have made a difference?

He'll never know.

Terry's relationship with his biological father hasn't wavered since their first meeting. When his daughter was moving and was short on helpers, his daughter suggested he ask his two dads if they'd be willing to help. To Terry's amazement, they both agreed.

Afterwards, Terry and his two dads went out for dinner and a few beers.

"It was heartwarming to see how well my two dads got along. They have so much in common. And not just that they were born three weeks apart in September 1949. They're an example of how good human beings should act with one another. They were proud that they had me in common. It wasn't a competition."

He adds, "I feel like I won the lottery for people who go through this. But that doesn't mean it's been easy. It hasn't."

Terry's forgiven his parents for hiding the truth of his conception.

He no longer feels like a dirty secret, but he still struggles when people ask him to share his story.

"Sometimes I just say I learned later in life I was adopted. That's my way of not having to deal with it. Sometimes I'm okay with it and sometimes I'm not. Sometimes I say, I'll share my story, but I don't know if it qualifies me to give a TED talk or be on the Jerry Springer show."

When I ask him about his lost Latino identity, he says, "I was so proud. I wish I could pull it back to me. But it's gone now. I can't have it back."

* * *

In a follow-up email Terry sends me photos of his family, and a particularly poignant photo of him and his two dads. Terry stands between them, their arms around each other. His biological dad leans one arm on a piano, his pose casual and nonchalant. His other dad, the father who raised him, sports a baseball cap and is grinning broadly.

He adds, "I felt a great affinity toward you while sharing our stories with one another."

I feel the same affinity in this peculiar community of unearthed family secrets.

PART II

Adoption

CHAPTER 12

Sealed Records and Primal Wounds

A Brief History of Adoption

In 1943, a young World War II soldier was desperately seeking information about his birth family. Stationed overseas, he wrote a series of letters to Ruth Brenner, director of the adoption agency that placed him, pleading for information about his natal origins. A few letters, which were posted on The Adoption History Project website, expressed the frustration that adoptees feel when looking for their birth parents, wrangling with adoption agencies and their strict code of confidentiality.

The unnamed soldier, who had become close to Brenner through their letters, called her "Godmother" and asked her to be executor of his will, in the event of his death—a dismaying request that reflected not only his closeness to Brenner but, possibly, his estrangement from his adoptive family. There is never any mention of them.

Regardless of their closeness, Brenner, though responding with empathy, would not violate the agency's confidentiality policies.

She wrote: "For the sake of the children, the agency asks parents not to expect to be told their whereabouts, and at the same time the agency agrees that information about parents will be kept confidential."[18]

In answer to Brenner's rejection of his request, the soldier further argued his case. "I believe I have a decent right to know more about and be free to call on members of my own family if I so chose."

Besides information about his birth parents, the soldier wanted information about blood relations. "I want to know also if I have any brothers or sisters. . . . I certainly intend to meet them."[19] He stated that it was necessity, not curiosity, that impelled him to make these requests.

Brenner never broke the seal of confidentiality. Perhaps playing amateur psychologist, she suggested that his earnestness in desiring this information was because he was experiencing unusual stress, and that each time he struggled or had a setback in life, he imagined that his unknown family would somehow be everything he longed for.

No doubt, as a soldier during war time, he was under undue stress. Yet, he discounted that as his reason for seeking his birth parents.

"For many years I have had one thought in mind. . . . and that is to learn more of my own business."[20]

Although he conceded that Brenner had certain responsibilities, he found her rules silly. In every letter, he pleaded with her to break this code of confidentiality. "Perhaps this time you will feel disposed to assist me in this matter. Perhaps you will not. But I should learn one day if I live. . . ."[21]

Questions of his origins must have preyed on the soldier's mental state as everyday he faced life and death life situations. *Who am I? Who are my people?* Maybe he was looking for something or someone to come home to.

Brenner never gave him the answers he was seeking. The young soldier died in China, never knowing who his birth parents were and who he was.

No one should die not knowing who their parents were and not being known to them, I thought after reading the letters.

However, even if the unnamed soldier lived, it's doubtful he would have found his birth parents or learned if he had brothers and/or sisters. Mrs. Brenner, as empathic as she was, was bound by state mandates about confidentiality. She was, as the saying goes, just following orders. These orders that were meant to protect adoption's triad—the birth parents, the adoptive parents, and the adoptee—even when the adult adoptee no longer needed or wanted protection.

Closed Adoptions and Sealed Records

To understand the rationale behind closed adoptions and sealed records, it's important to examine when these protocols began and why. The earliest record of a state mandating sealed records was at the beginning of the twentieth century.

"In 1917 . . . Minnesota passed the first state law that required children and adults to be investigated and adoption records to be shielded from public view."[22]

The reasoning behind closing the court records to public inspection was to protect the privacy of all participants in the adoption process. However, at that time, children and adults who were directly involved in the adoption process were still allowed access to the records. But that changed beginning in the 1930s.

"[I]n the 1930s, 1940s, and early 1950s, virtually all states took the further step of imposing a unitary regime of secrecy under which adopting parents and birth parents who were unknown to one another would remain unknown and under which adult adoptees could never learn the identity of their birth parents."[23]

Additionally, by mid-century, most states had revised their laws to incorporate minimum standards, such as pre-placement inquiry, post-placement probation, as well as confidentiality and sealed records.[24] Thus, after World War II, information about birth families was placed off-limits to adoptees in most US states.[25] In effect, these laws, which had become the rule rather than the exception, obliterated the adopted person's birth identity.

If protecting the parties involved in the adoption was the reason for sealing the records from the public, what were the states protecting them from? Why did most states take the further step of sealing the records from the involved parties?

What prompted states to seal records from the public was the stigma associated with illegitimacy. Banning a nosy neighbor or family member from accessing an adoptee's records shielded the child from being labeled a bastard. Also, sealing the records prevented birth parents from interfering with or harassing adoptive parents and their adopted children.[26]

Besides sealing the records, certain states took a further step to ensure confidentiality and to prevent birth parents' interference by issuing adoptees new birth certificates, which listed the adoptive parents as the birth parents. Not only did the new birth certificate erase the adoptee's original identity, it also fostered the illusion that the adoptive parents were the birth parents. The original birth certificates with the natal parents, or at least the birth mothers, were sealed away, making it virtually impossible for adoptees to uncover their natal identity.[27]

Brad Ewell, an adoptee whose story appears in Chapter 13, describes the confusion he experienced when comparing his birth certificate with his wife's, who was not adopted. What prompted him to compare the two birth certificates was that after he'd made his DNA results public on a genealogical site, an unknown woman contacted him.

The woman claimed to be his maternal aunt. Brad had no idea who the woman was, but he wanted to reassure her that he wasn't her nephew. However, when he compared his birth certificate to his wife's, he was baffled. His birth certificate had been altered in ways that suggested it was a copy. His father hadn't signed the certificate. Instead, his name was typed in. In the place of the hospital's name was a dash.

He was told by another adoptee that if he wanted to unseal his adoption records, he would need a court order. Additionally, he'd have only one chance to appear before a judge to petition to have his records opened. If his petition failed, he wouldn't be eligible for a second chance. Luckily for Brad, he had other resources available to him in his search for his birth family.

"Matching" was another paradigm mandated by most states, which promised a seamless integration of the child into the adoptive family, until the late 1960s.

According to Ellen Herman, author of *Kinship by Design*, "matching required that adoptive parents be married heterosexuals who looked, felt, and believed as if they had, by themselves, conceived other people's children. The idea was that matching would encourage autonomous and permanent kinship."[28]

To achieve that goal, there should be a "physical resemblance, intellectual similarity, and a racial and religious continuity between parents and children."[29]

Most of the adoptees I interviewed either weren't matched or if they were matched, said that they still were aware of physical and/ or temperament differences between themselves and their adoptive parents.

In matching racially ambiguous children with adoptive parents, white adoption professionals considered adoption all but impossible for these children.

Herman states: "Placement across race lines was unthinkable even in cases where it might be invisible."[30]

To Tell or Not to Tell, That Is the Question

If sealed records and matching were strategies meant to ensure integration of adoptees into adoptive families, whether to tell the adoptees they were adopted posed a gray area. On one hand, telling adoptees prevented them from learning about their adoptions from a relative, neighbor, or classmate; on the other, it presented a psychological risk to the adoptee. Even though adoption professionals provided guidance on how to tell adoptees they were adopted, stressing that they were a chosen child, the act of telling adoptees revealed that they'd been given away by their birth parents, which they might perceive as a rejection.[31]

By the 1950s, many adoption agencies must have come to the conclusion that it was more beneficial to tell because they required that adopters pledge in writing that they would tell the child that he or she was adopted. Regardless of the written pledge, it's estimated that a considerable number of adoptees were never told.[32]

For adoptees who weren't told they were adopted, imagine the shock when they discover as adults, either through a DNA test or a well-intentioned relative, that both their parents aren't their birth parents?

Adult discovery adoptee, Susan McCrea, found out that she was adopted in a circuitous way. Rather than tell Susan directly, her nephew opted to break the shocking news to her husband, leaving him with the unenviable task of upending his wife's life. The reason the nephew gave for revealing this long-held family secret was that he felt she had the right to know. Needless to say, the revelation sent her into a tailspin. When she confronted her adoptive mother, she confirmed it was true.

Susan described the process of finding her birth mother as intricate, spanning a twenty-year period, due in part to the difficulty of getting her adoption records. If she had known as a child that she was adopted, once she became an adult she might have started her search sooner, and possibly had more time with her birth mother. By the time Susan was able to finally connect with her birth mother, she was sixty and her birthmother was eighty.

My close friend and colleague, Linda Landis Andrews, who never knew she was adopted, learned of her adoption from her adoptive mother during an emotional outburst. Toward the end of her mother's life, she suffered from Alzheimer's disease and in a moment of frustration with Linda, she blurted out, "I took you in when nobody wanted you."

"I was a cute little kid. Lots of people would have wanted me," Linda answered.

"No," her mother protested. "Your mother was a barfly. And nobody wanted you."

I asked Linda if she realized the full import of her mother's words at the time of the revelation.

"Yes," she said. "I knew she was saying that I wasn't her daughter."

To find out in such a blinding way that your mother isn't your mother and have the confidence and presence of mind to defend yourself amazes me.

This surprising disclosure began a difficult and sometimes baffling journey to find her birth parents. Unfortunately, Linda discovered that her birth parents and her two birth sisters were deceased. However, she was able to connect with her two birth sisters' families. And the sister Linda grew up with, who she believed was her blood sister, had also been adopted. In her long search for identity and family, Linda would also discover a half-sister on her paternal side, who she connected with and is now a part of her life.

If Linda had known she was adopted, she might have met her two sisters, who were raised by their mutual mother, and learned about the mother she'd never known.

The Collision of Morality and Sexuality

Sealed records, altered birth certificates, and, in many cases, nondisclosure marked adoptions after World War II, just as the number of adoptions skyrocketed. Historians refer to this time period as the Baby Scoop Era, spanning the late 1940s to approximately 1972. The Baby Scoop Era was "characterized by an increased rate of premarital pregnancies . . . along with a higher rate of newborn adoptions. It is estimated that up to 4 million mothers in the United States surrendered newborn babies to adoption; 2 million during the 1960s alone."[33] Many of those

4 million babies would never discover their natal parents. Some would never even know they were adopted.

Ann Fessler, author of *The Girls Who Went Away*, attributes this sharp increase in unmarried pregnant women to two factors: "a liberalization of sexual mores combined with restrictions on access to birth control." Fessler states that it wouldn't be until 1970 that "most women, whether married or single, were able to get prescriptions for the pill or other contraceptive devices."[34]

Relatively more of these unmarried pregnant women came from white middle-class families. According to Professor Ellen Herman, "their mortified parents desperately wanted their daughters to have another chance at marriage and 'normal' motherhood. To guard the identities of the disgraced birth mothers and shield the adoptees from information that might shock them, confidentiality gradually calcified into secrecy,"[35] a secrecy that many of these women and their families took to their graves—or intended to.

The psychological and social work view, which supported the parents' viewpoint, was that these women were better off surrendering their newborns. It was the best option for all involved parties. No help was given to them. In fact, they were coerced by their parents to give up their children and move on with their lives. They were deemed "trash" and shunned by society.[36] With no help from their parents, and possibly wanting to shed the stain of societal shame, what choice did they have but to capitulate and surrender their children? Meanwhile, their male counterparts escaped societal condemnation and shaming.

Although I understand the religious and societal factors that influenced many embarrassed parents to pressure their daughters to surrender their babies, one question puzzles me: Did these parents ever consider that they were giving away their grandchildren?

These unwed mothers were shipped off to maternity homes to give birth and surrender their babies for adoption. Once the baby was surrendered, then the young woman could get on with her life, as if it had never happened. Her privacy and the privacy of her child were protected by the closed adoption and the sealed records, which meant that there was no way for her child to find her or for her to find her child. It was as if her child had died.

But with the proliferation of commercial DNA tests, these well-buried secrets have erupted, shaking the foundations of adoptees' sense of self, and presenting the possibility for adoptees to reunite with their birth mothers. Even if the adoptee had a wonderful and caring upbringing, many want to know the truth of their identities.

As David Brodzinsky, professor emeritus of clinical psychology at Rutgers University, who studied the psychological issues within the adoption and foster care systems, states: "The desire to know more about one's birth family is normal. Part of the universal search for self."[37] Wanting to know their birth parents is not only normal but part of the process of piecing together their shattered identities.

For adoptees in many states, the obstacle of sealed records remains. However, unlike the World War II soldier who had no resources to help him find his birth parents, adoptees today do. Ironically, the very tool that uncovers adoption secrets also, in some instances, helps to locate the birth parents through familial DNA matches.

Additionally, in the intervening years after the implementation of closed adoptions and sealed records, various groups and organizations have formed to help adoptees and birth parents unite, including Orphan Voyage (1953); the Adoptees Liberty Movement Association (1971); the International Soundex Reunion Registry, a mutual consent registry that requires the consent of both parties (adoptees and birth mothers and/or birth parents) (1975); and Bastard Nation (1996).

Even the National Council for Adoption, that once opposed unrestricted access to sealed records, has softened its stance and now supports legislation that balances the needs of adult adoptees and their birth parents.[38]

However, the fact that not all birth mothers want to be found by their surrendered children endures. Many did what their parents wanted them to do—got on with their lives and tried to forget. Some married, some had children. Some never told their husbands or children that they'd had a child out of wedlock, who they'd surrendered. After all, they were reassured that their privacy would be protected. To have that individual suddenly appear in their lives not only brings back that painful and gut-wrenching experience, but it disrupts the life they've created. They also may have regrets over the relinquishment or be suspicious of the adopted individual, who is practically a stranger.[39]

In the adoptees' desire to find and connect with their birth parents, they risk being rejected by their birth parents. From the adoptees' perspective, the birth parents' refusal of a relationship with them may reinforce their initial feelings of abandonment. Additionally, seeking their birth parents, there's the added risk that their adoptive parents might feel threatened and/or hurt. All of these potential issues complicate an adoptee's need for connection with their birth parents but, nonetheless, don't negate the adoptee's psychological desire to know who they are.

Primal Wounds

After doing extensive research on adoption, adoptee Dr. Jack Rocco (Chapter 15), who always knew he was adopted, now believes that his separation from his mother after his birth caused trauma. He's not alone in his belief. According to some psychologists, adoptees do experience separation from their mothers as trauma, sometimes referred to as "a primal wound."

Nancy Verrier, author of *The Primal Wound: Understanding the Adopted Child*, describes the primal wound as "a wound which is physical, emotional, psychological, and spiritual, a wound which causes pain so profound as to have been described as cellular by those adoptees who allowed themselves to go that deeply into their pain."[40]

Verrier further explains that "[w]hen this natural evolution is interrupted by a postnatal separation from the biological mother, the resultant experience of abandonment and loss is indelibly imprinted upon the unconscious minds of these children, causing that which I call the 'primal wound.'"[41]

Paul Sunderland, a psychologist who specializes in trauma and has a particular interest in adoptees, categorizes the trauma that the infant experiences as a remembered trauma, not a recalled trauma. Since the trauma is preverbal, it can't be recalled, but it can be remembered.[42]

In analyzing the adoption experiences, Sunderland believes that the term adoption does not accurately describe what it is—a relinquishment. For society, the word adoption is a form of denial. The term "relinquishment" better reflects what happens to all the involved parties—not just the adopted child, but the birth parents and the adoptive parents, who also experience trauma. Sunderland calls this the triangle of adoption.

For the adoptee, the issue of abandonment is life-threatening. Is there a bigger life threat than being separated from one's mother as an infant? Then adoptees enter a family that doesn't genetically fit them, and many have the impossible task of having to be someone that they could never be and having to fix the adoptive parents' wounds. As Sunderland points out, for the adoptive parents, infertility is an enormous grief. Is it any wonder that adoptees are overrepresented in mental health settings?[43]

For people adopted thirty to fifty years ago, many have the added stress of coming to the adoptive family with no idea of their history, and they're not legally allowed to find out. (Not until the 1990s would open adoptions become more common practice in the US, which allowed the adoptees access to their family history.)[44]

Sunderland asks the question that strikes at the heart of the adoptee's psyche: If the first most important person gives me up, how do I know the next one won't?

The birth parents also suffer trauma. They usually say not a day goes by that they don't think about what happened. And the adoptive parents suffer the trauma of not being able to have children.

Relinquishment of a child is a three-pronged grief. The grief of the child who's been waiting nine months to meet his or her mother. The grief of the adoptive parents who can't have a child. And the grief of the mother who gave up her child.[45]

Jack Rocco, who eventually found his birth mother, said that to his knowledge he had approximately fifteen minutes with his birth mother. And that was it. Then six weeks in an orphanage before his parents adopted him.

After Susan McCrea discovered she was adopted, she tracked down the agency that handled her adoption. At that time, the agency had a policy due to health concerns—that newborns were not to be held. She thinks her birth mother was never permitted to hold her. Sixty years after Susan's birth, she finally met her birth mother, and for the first time, she was embraced by her.

Adding to the trauma of relinquishment is guilt.

As Nancy Verrier states: "Whereas the birth mother may feel guilty for giving up her baby, the adoptive mother feels guilty for somehow failing to adequately take her place. *The child feels guilty for having been born.*"[46]

As impactful as the primal wound theory is, it's been suggested that it fosters victimhood in adoptees. If adoptees believe they were wounded by adoption, they may become stuck in this psychological trauma, seeing themselves as scarred.

Adoptee and psychologist Marcy Axness counters that argument. Although she agrees that treating adoptees as victims cripples them, she also thinks that only by facing the loss of the birth mother and grieving that loss will the adoptee be able to integrate and heal.

"This . . . is what effective healing work is about: not 'fixing' it, but facing it."[47] As with any loss, first, you have to acknowledge it before you can integrate it into your life. And to acknowledge that loss, you obviously need to know what you've lost. Or rather, who you've lost. You need to know your origin story.

Sealed Records Today

Bastard Nation, an organization dedicated to the recognition of the full human and civil right of adult adoptees, is militant in its stance that every adoptee has the right to their official birth records, unaltered and free from falsification. Their mission statement asserts that they have reclaimed "the badge of bastardy" placed on them by those who would attempt to shame them. They see nothing shameful in having been born out of wedlock or being adopted.[48]

As of the writing of this book, according to Bastard Nation, only fifteen states allow adult adoptees to have unrestricted access to their own original birth records: Alabama, Alaska, Connecticut, Colorado, Kansas, Louisiana, Maine, Massachusetts, Minnesota, New Hampshire, New York, Oregon, Rhode Island, South Dakota, and Vermont.

But certain states, such as Illinois, allow restricted access to adoptees' birth certificates. As stated in Illinois's amended 2010 adoption policy, it "recognizes the basic right of all persons to access their birth records and, to this end, supports public policy that allows an adult adoptee access to his or her original birth certificate." However, it also says that it acknowledges that there may be circumstances where the birth parents wish to remain anonymous. To balance these two disparate wishes, the birth certificate will be released to the adult adoptee "unless a request for anonymity has been filed with the Registry by a birth parent named on the original birth certificate."[49] In other words, if a birth parent doesn't want to be found and files a request for anonymity, the adoptee will never know his or her birth parents.

Contrary to the United States, the United Kingdom has enacted laws enabling adoptees over the age of eighteen to see their sealed records. Besides being over eighteen, everyone adopted before November 12, 1975 has to attend a counselling session with an approved adoption adviser first before they are able to access their records.[50]

Whether the remaining states continue to restrict access to original birth certificates, the fact remains: As more and more adults who were adopted take DNA tests, the truth of their origins won't remain secret.

CHAPTER 13

Not the Father He Expected

Brad Ewell: Plano, Texas

BRAD EWELL'S FAMILY STORY IS INKED INTO HIS SKIN. THAT'S HOW DEEP IT goes for him.

On his right wrist YOU GO is tattooed. WE GO graces his wife's left wrist. When they hold hands, the tattoos read, YOU GO, WE GO—a line from the movie *Back Draft* about catching someone and never letting go. The tattoos would prove prophetic.

On his other wrist is a small F4 Phantom symbol, a tribute to his adoptive dad who was a fighter pilot during the Vietnam War. The F4 was his favorite plane.

However, the tattoo that cuts the deepest is the heart pierced by a dagger. Surrounding the heart are four roses and a banner that says: FAMILY. The four roses represent both sets of his parents and his recently found four half siblings. The heart tattoo sits above YOU GO, as if the words are a buffer, a soft place to land, a reminder that his wife is there for him.

"I got this one after my discovery," Brad explains the daggered heart. "My family is something I'd fight to the death for. Family is also something that has pierced my heart. I'm not sure I'll ever recover."

As a police sergeant and a bomb squad commander, Brad has fought for justice his entire adult life. Then, at forty-eight, he had a DNA surprise that is the stuff of Hollywood movies. Not only was Brad adopted, but his biological father is a murderer.

In the murky and mysterious journeys of adoptees, no one expects or is prepared for such a destabilizing discovery.

I Keep Telling Myself This Is a Mistake

On a Zoom call, Brad unspools his incredible story from his bedroom. His thick shock of gray hair and full beard threaded with gray gives him a rugged appearance, as do the tattoos that festoon his forearms. But underneath his imposing exterior is a man who, as he tells it, is still riven to the core by his family secret.

On the evening that derailed his life, his wife and her parents were untangling their own family tree.

But Brad didn't join them. Something was eating at him. At lunch, his wife told him a woman had contacted her via Facebook messenger claiming to be a relative, possibly his maternal aunt. She'd seen his DNA results posted on Ancestry.

Brad dismissed her claim. First, he had no idea who this woman was. Second, he looked just like his mom. Everyone always said so.

But still something niggled at him.

Maybe his grandmother had been telling the truth. On her death-bed, she'd confessed to Brad's mother that she'd been adopted.

"I kind of regret it." she said, in a particularly brutal manner. "I did it because your daddy wanted to."

Since his grandmother was sick at the time, Brad hadn't put too much stock in her deathbed confession. As he listened to his wife and her parents in the next room, he decided to put his suspicions to rest.

"I also wanted to help the woman by eliminating me from her list of potential nephews," Brad says.

The fact that he and this woman's nephew shared the same birth date and place of birth was a coincidence. Lots of people shared birth dates and birth places. To be certain, Brad dug out his wife's and his birth certificates to compare them, because they'd both been born in Dallas in 1970.

"The birth certificates couldn't have been more different. Mine looked like an old microfiche copy," he explains.

The most perplexing inconsistency was the absence of a hospital listed on his birth certificate; it was just a dash. Unlike his wife's birth certificate, which was signed by her father, Brad's had his father's name typed in. Additionally, his wife's birth certificate was stamped with the Dallas County seal and Brad's was stamped with the Travis County seal.

Tamping down his panic, he struggled to find a logical reason for the discrepancies in the birth certificates.

"I told myself, my parents lost my birth certificate. And that this was a copy."

Looking at the two birth certificates, he began thinking about the woman's description and location of the women's clinic where the baby was born. The unknown woman had relayed these facts to his wife.

That's when he freaked out. He realized that he'd been to that clinic before.

"When we visited my grandparents, my parents often took me to see a doctor at that clinic," Brad says.

Panicked, but still clinging to the belief it was a mistake, he googled the clinic's location. Within seconds, he was looking at a white brick building with a green roof that he recognized.

He jokes that as a cop he's always hearing from perps that their wrongdoing was a big misunderstanding. Yet, that was what he was thinking—it was a big misunderstanding. However, the more he stared at the building, the more he realized that this was not good.

Not wanting to bring his in-laws into this emotional whirlwind yet, he sat and stewed.

Once his in-laws left, he told his wife what he discovered—the discrepancies in their birth certificates and that as a child, he'd visited the location where the Facebook woman's nephew had been born.

The questions he'd been asking himself, he asked his wife.

"My mom and dad were at the birth of our three kids. Tell me one story you've ever heard about the day I was born," he questioned.

She paused for a moment before answering. "I don't think your mom ever told any."

"Tell me anything she told you about being pregnant with me."

She couldn't think of any.

"Okay, one last thing," he said. "My parents took pictures of everything back then. Have you ever seen a picture of my mom pregnant?"

"I've never seen one," she responded.

"Neither have I."

They sat in silence, stunned and confused.

"What should I do?" Brad asked. "I don't want to ask my parents. What if it's a mistake? I don't want to upset them."

"How about contacting Ann? You know, the woman from our church who's always known she was adopted," his wife suggested.

Within three days, everything Brad thought he knew about himself was changed forever.

We've Been Trying to Find a Way to Tell You

"I don't think you're going to like what I have to say," Ann told him. As Brad's wife had advised, he contacted Ann, thinking she might shed light on his confusing birth certificate.

When Ann called, Brad was at the police station, sitting at his desk. He confesses he doesn't know what he was doing at work. His mind was a muddle.

She told him that based on his birth certificate and additional research into Texas adoptees' birth certificates, she concluded that he'd been adopted.

To support her conclusion, she texted him a picture of her birth certificate for comparison. Same microfiche appearance, a dash for the birth location, no father's signature, and it was stamped with the Travis County seal—just like Brad's.

"This is what an adoptee's birth certificate looked like in Texas in the seventies," she said.

His mind racing, he asked her about unsealing his adoption records. She explained that you were at the mercy of whatever judge you found yourself in front of.

"You can present all the reasons they should unseal the records and the judge can say no. As soon as the judge says no, you're done."

Brad shrugged his shoulders in disgust.

"That's why I didn't pursue it."

Three hours after talking to Ann, Brad called his dad on his cellphone, thinking he'd leave him a message about grabbing a coffee sometime. His plan was to defer that tough conversation until he could get his head together.

"He almost never answers his cellphone," Brad says. "But he did that day."

Not wanting to have the conversation on the phone while his father was driving, Brad skirted the issue.

"I've got a couple of things I'm working on and the next time you're around, let's get together and talk."

"Yeah, sure. Why do you want to talk?" his father asked.

"I told him it was nothing urgent. But he wasn't having it."

His father pressed the issue. "I want to know what you want. I don't like walking into anything blind."

Brad wonders if his father was suspicious, because he knew about the DNA test he'd recently taken. Yet, neither parent had said a word to him about being adopted.

Finally, Brad told him everything.

"She thinks I'm that baby. Y'all never told me I was adopted."

"Huh," was his father's only response.

The silence between them was broken only by his father's fingers drumming on the car's steering wheel.

"I guess from being a cop, 'huh' was all I needed. Even though it wasn't an answer, it was an answer. My heart broke."

"I said to him, 'You know dad, I'm not trying to be a dick here, but I need you to say it. I know I'm adopted, but I need you to say it to make it real.'"

His dad sighed and said, "Yeah, you're adopted. We've been trying to find a way to tell you."

"He's been trying for forty-eight years to tell me? That was the new lie," Brad says, scoffing at his father's excuse.

His father ended the conversation saying that none of that matters because they loved him and were still his parents. And that he needed to go home and tell his wife.

Brad interrupts his narrative and expresses the anguish experienced by so many people who've uncovered similar family secrets.

"Hearing my dad say 'none of it matters' is still a trigger for me. The only reason it doesn't matter to somebody is because they've never been through it. It absolutely matters when you wake up one day and you find out you're not the kid of the people who raised you. It's three years now, and I still struggle with it."

Brad is convinced that his adoptive parents were never going to tell him he was adopted.

"I firmly believe they were taking it to their graves."

Later, when he questioned them both about their secrecy, they claimed that they were told not to tell him, because it would make him sad. And they didn't want him to be sad. Brad doesn't buy that. Also, their explanation isn't supported by adoption protocol in the 1970s, when Brad was adopted. Many states required adoptive parents to sign a form pledging to tell the child of the adoption.

He thinks one of the reasons they didn't tell him was his mom's insecurities. In her mind, there can be only one mom. And she needed that mom to be her.

"It sucks for me. If you're not ready to deal with that, then maybe adoption's not the thing for you," he says.

It's a harsh statement, but it speaks to the depth of Brad's hurt and anger about his parents' secrecy. Whether right or wrong, it's not unusual for some adoptive parents to be reluctant to discuss the adoption. After all, they were promised a sealed adoption. Then suddenly, they're confronted with a secret they believed would never be revealed and that was legally protected.

This reluctance goes both ways, though. Relinquishing parents also may not want to be contacted by their natural child, disturbing their established lives and possibly shining an unfavorable light on their characters.

I ask him if he feels betrayed by them.

He doesn't hesitate. "Sure."

After Brad's adoption was confirmed by his father, he was in no condition to talk to his newly discovered aunt.

"Everything about myself was wrong. Though I still had the same job, same kids, same wife, same house. Nothing had changed. But at the same time, everything in my life had changed."

He asked his wife to be his go-between, filtering the information from his aunt about his biological parents.

Several days later, he changed his mind. He told his wife, he wanted to know everything about his birth parents.

"You're not ready," she said protectively. She knew how explosive the information would be for him.

"Now I had to know," he says. "That's when I found out my biological dad was Jimmie Graves. And that he was in prison for murder."

Jimmie Ray Graves: Not the Father Brad Expected

Jimmie Ray Graves's backward slide into crime began when he quit his junior draftsman job because he was passed over for a senior draftsman position. He not only wasn't given the promotion but had to train the new senior draftsman. After that, he began working in bars and strip clubs—places motorcycle gangs hung out. He always loved motorcycles. So, it wasn't long before he became a member of the violent motorcycle and drug gang called the Bandidos.

"We're the people your parents warned you about," reads an old Bandidos motto. They pride themselves on being the baddest of the bad.

In 1972, two years after Brad was born, Graves killed a National Guard sergeant with two bullets to the back of his head on Interstate 20 in Caddo Parish in Louisiana. The guard, Charles Overfield, had interrupted a burglary at a National Guard armory in Shreveport and was set to testify against one of the suspects, Robert Powell, a Bandidos associate.

After Graves was apprehended, he pleaded guilty to avoid the death penalty and was given a life sentence in Angola State Penitentiary in Louisiana.[51] Built on a former slave plantation, Angola has the dubious distinction of being nicknamed the Alcatraz of the South and has a reputation for brutality and violence.[52]

At the time of Brad's discovery, Graves was one of the longest-serving inmates in Angola State Penitentiary. Upon learning of his biological father's criminal past, Brad's first thought was if he ever spoke to him—*a big if*—it would be a one-and-done. He'd dealt with criminals and knew how their conversation would go. *Nothing is my fault. The world is against me. I didn't do anything wrong. These bad things happened to me because I have bad luck."*

After six months of psychotherapy, prompted by watching an NBC *Dateline* episode on Angola that kept him sleepless for three nights, Brad decided to meet his biological father. He came to the conclusion that he'd have regrets if he never met him. At the time, Graves was in his mid-seventies and had already survived a heart attack.

"I was struggling with my identity. You know, who the hell am I? I needed to lay eyes on someone that was directly responsible for my existence on earth."

Nothing about Brad's meeting with his natural father went as expected.

"He walked in, gave me a hug, and said, 'Son, it's good to meet you.' Then within two to three minutes of meeting, he said that he intentionally meant to kill Overfield and that it was all his fault. He just owned it."

When Brad tells me this, he opens his eyes wide and leans toward the screen to show his surprise. His biological father's admission of guilt was a game changer for him. He says the room reminded him of an old church meeting room, with a beige tile floor and white walls.

They talked for eight hours—while in the background electronic locks buzzed, doors and gates slammed shut, and prisoners came and went.

Graves told Brad about his life in prison: how he'd escaped once and been caught; the things he'd done to sustain himself in there; the good things he'd done; and about his heart attack ten years ago. A widow maker.

"And I told him my life story. That's when he said he had no idea I existed. He knew my mom was pregnant, but they weren't exclusive back then. But seeing me, he knew I was his."

I ask Brad if he saw a resemblance between him and his natural father.

"Oh, God, yes. I'm built just like him. And we share personality traits, which I never shared with my adoptive parents. For one, I'm more introverted like him."

Brad looks off to the side, collecting his thoughts.

"One of the best things mental health–wise for me was to finally see *me* back in someone else."

University of Chicago Professor Gina Miranda Samuels (Crown School of Social Work, Policy, and Practice) points out the importance of looking like your family for familial belonging.

"In U.S. culture, the dominant frame for legitimizing kinship ties is through one's resemblance to other family members in physical and personal traits. . . . [I]n this way, we authenticate our sense of self, familial belonging, and very existence."[53]

In a follow up email, Brad writes about the importance of genetic mirroring to his healing—a concept that many of the people I interviewed talked about.

"People take for granted growing up with people that they're related to who look like them. I didn't have that with my adoptive parents. But I had it when I met my bio-dad. To this day, it's still hard to put into words. After a year of not knowing who I was, seeing him let me feel whole and real again."

You Will Always Be My Dad

As life-altering and healing as Brad's prison visit with his biological father was, he didn't feel comfortable sharing it with his adoptive parents. He knew they didn't want to hear about it. Whenever biological stuff about his birth family came up, his parents changed the subject—a strategy my mother used when I sought information about our mixed-race family. So, Brad kept his visit with his bio-dad a secret.

It wasn't until his adoptive father was in the hospital dying that he was able to share with him what he'd learned about his biological family.

The week before he died, Brad spent a night with him in the hospital. His dad, who was having trouble breathing, was on a B-Pap machine. When he woke up in the middle of the night, he began fighting to get the mask off. After Brad removed the mask, his dad reminded him that he had a DNR ("Do not resuscitate" directive).

"Don't let them do that crap to me," he said.

After Brad assured him he wouldn't let that happen, out of the blue, his father piped up: "Brad, tell me about your biological family. Have you met?"

Protective of his father's ill health, Brad chose his words carefully.

"Dad, I thought you didn't like to talk about that."

"No, I do. It was just your mother is always around. And I didn't want to upset her."

Brad hesitated, then said, "We met about a month ago."

His father's response stunned him.

"That's great. I'm glad you finally got to meet your dad."

"I stopped him and said, 'You will always be my dad.'"

For the next hour, they talked about his adoption. Nothing specific. It was just his dad finally acknowledging what had been going on in Brad's life. By the time they were done talking, his dad was nodding off.

"In my head, it was truly a lifesaver," Brad says.

About a week later, his adoptive father died.

He tells me that he's taken to calling his biological father "Pop" because it recognizes their bond, but still leaves a place for the dad who raised him.

As for his adoptive mother, who now has Alzheimer's, she's incapable of telling him anything about his adoption, but she remains staunch in her belief that keeping his adoption secret from him was the right thing to do.

"We just don't talk about it," Brad says.

I Was Just Not Spoken of Again

From Brad's maternal aunt, he learned that she was the only family member who knew of his existence. At the time of his birth mother's pregnancy, she was living with her sister. Fearing retribution from her father, his birth mother hid her pregnancy from her parents. But her secrecy didn't stop there. After she married, she never told her husband of thirty years or her two children that she'd had another child. Brad also has a half-brother on his biological father's side.

To my surprise, Brad says, "The only person's decision-making I never questioned in this whole thing was my bio-mom giving me up for adoption."

It's not what I expected to hear. In Brad's mind, his birth mother giving him up made sense to him, but his adoptive parents' secrecy didn't.

"I don't see any way out of this that worked well for her," Brad says of his birth mother.

At eighteen, with no husband and no means of support, his biological mom relinquished him two days after he was born. It's not until he talked to his half-sister, who he refers to as his sister, did he fully understand how his relinquishment affected his birth mom.

Although she never told anyone about him, she never forgot him.

"My sister's father was in the military. And the fourth of July was a big deal in their family. But every fourth, my birth mom would turn into a recluse. She wouldn't go out for a week. She told her family, 'You all go camping. Do what you want to do. I just need a little time.'"

"You see, my birthday is July 8th," Brad explains. "She did this every year. She mourned me until the day she died."

Brad's biological mother died in 2002 at forty-nine, nineteen years before his discovery.

"My aunt said the day after I was born, she left the hospital, and I left the hospital. I was just not spoken of again."

But he was never far from her thoughts. When his sister was diagnosed with cancer, his birth mom said to her, "This is a curse. It's because of me. I can't explain it. I'm so sorry."

Until the day she died, his birth mom felt guilty for relinquishing him.

"She took a lot of guilt to her grave," Brad says. "Never told a soul about me."

I stop the video and jot a note to myself. Not so much to remember what I'm feeling, but to release the emotions Brad's story is triggering in me.

I write: "I'm finding it hard transcribing Brad's interview, listening again to his story, the way people's lives spin out, and the collateral damage it causes."

In a year, these words would come to haunt me, when my life once again spins out of my control.

What should take me several more days to transcribe, takes me another week. *Is it just his story? Or is it the accumulation of these stories that plunge me into sadness?*

The Hardest Part

For Brad, one of the hardest parts of navigating his discovery was feeling abandoned by his adoptive parents when they wouldn't participate in his reunion journey.

"That's when I needed them more than any other time in my life. In trying to do any kind of reunion journey and feeling so bitter about secrets, and then finding yourself having to keep secrets because they don't want to hear about it, was brutal."

Then Brad references the primal wound, a concept I didn't expect him to discuss.

"If you talk to enough adoptees, and I have, we all end up growing up the same. Because of that primal wound of losing your mom, you're constantly trying to please the people who adopted you. You're constantly afraid they're going to disappear."

Then he shifts gears. What he says next feels like a physical blow.

"Lost time is the second hardest part of this discovery. I can never meet my biological mother. Never going to happen. She was gone nineteen years before I knew she existed."

He takes a deep breath.

"And my sister, who I've grown super close to, was diagnosed in

2019 with stage 4 ovarian cancer. She's in the palliative stage right now. They've given all the chemo they can give her. Whenever it comes raging back, there's nothing they can do. Best-case scenario, a couple more years with her. She's the one I really clicked with. And she's the one I get the least amount of time with. The lost time has been really hard."

I stop the video again and make another note, perhaps to capture the moment accurately. Maybe I need a break from the sorrow I see on his face.

He's ironically stoical in his delivery, layered with profound sadness. If he has anger, it's not visible.

The Ending Not Expected

After that first meeting with Pop, Brad maintained contact with him, getting to know the man who'd given him life.

The upshot of their burgeoning relationship was as surprising as it was ironic. Brad decided to fight for Pop's release from prison.

Brad admits that he wouldn't have done it if Graves wasn't his biological father. But it wasn't just that.

"What the system did to him wasn't fair. He took a plea deal and then the state of Louisiana changed the terms of that agreement three times without him having any say in the matter."

Although Brad acknowledges that his biological father was a man who needed to go to prison for what he did, he doesn't believe he's the same man. His crime is over fifty years old. On behalf of his biological father, Brad went before the Louisiana House and Senate committees and pleaded for his release. He described Jimmy Graves as a success story.

Brad freely admits that others might not see it the way he does, and that his career in law enforcement carries a heavy irony. It also carried a heavy influence with the committees.

On November 17, 2022, Jimmie Graves was released from prison. Brad got to spend several days with him in Louisiana. Then, on December 6, 2022, Brad picked Pop up from a transitional program and brought him to Texas to stay with him and his family.

Brad emails me a photo of Pop and him sitting on Brad's front porch swing. Over their heads are an array of wind chimes. Jimmie wears an Army Veteran baseball cap. Their arms touch and their easy smiles tell their own story of family and redemption.

I email him back and ask what Jimmie's plans are going forward, wondering if he'll permanently reside with Brad and his family.

December 28, 2022.
Hey Gail,
The plans for now are him living in the house his friend has offered him and settling in on Parole.

I'm happy for Brad and Pop. But it's a bittersweet ending. Time lost never to be gotten back.

Better Off Knowing, or Not Knowing?

After transcribing Brad's interview, I email him follow-up questions, one of which is: "Knowing what you know now, would it have been better for you if you never knew you were adopted?"

His answer illuminates the dilemma faced by adults who make these startling discoveries.

On the one hand, I was happily living my life clueless about the reality of my biological roots. On the other hand, knowing I'm adopted has brought some really amazing people into my life. It's hard to imagine life without them. And knowing my biological roots has made me feel more grounded and more of a whole person than I ever had before. When I lean into these roots it brings me a great deal of personal peace. But that personal peace came at the cost of breaking a part of me that will never be fully whole again. So that's a lot of words to say, I really don't know.

While I appreciate the honesty of his answer, I can't help but wonder: *If Brad had known as a child that he was adopted, and if he'd been able to reunite with his mother, would he have answered differently?* It's impossible to know.

CHAPTER 14

___

A Confusion of Race

Dr. Verda Byrd: Converse, Texas

FOR THE FIRST SEVENTY YEARS OF VERDA BYRD'S LIFE, SHE WAS A BLACK woman. Then in 2013, Verda came across some disquieting papers. One was an adoption paper. The other was a Missouri birth certificate for a Jeanette Beagle, which didn't have a birth date. Verda had no idea who Jeanette Beagle was.

Three months later, she got the shock of her life.

*   *   *

In 2015, college instructor and president of the local chapter of Spokane, Washington's NAACP, Rachel Dolezal created a national controversy over her assertion of a Black identity. Although she was born to white parents, as documented by her white parents, she presented herself as a Black woman. In the midst of the controversy, she resigned as President of the NAACP in Seattle and was dismissed from her teaching position.

If it hadn't been for Rachel Dolezal's false claim that she was Black, Verda Byrd's unusual story might never have made national and international news.

As Verda explains why Dolezal's claim of Blackness prompted her to go to the media, even eight years later, I can hear the anger in her voice.

"It made me so angry that the next day I called the Channel 5 TV station in San Antonio and told them to get a reporter to my house. Because I had a story for them. I said, 'She was white and wanted to be Black. But I was born white and raised Black.'"

Verda smiles.

"The next day a reporter came to my house. Within twenty-four hours, my story went viral. 'A Black Woman Says She's White,'" she pauses.

"Regardless of who Rachel Dolezal was or who she wants to be, when you want to be something you're not, and you're not telling the truth about it, that made me angry. I wanted to tell my side of the race story."

But telling your side of the race story sometimes comes with public shaming, as I discovered myself. Verda admits that she didn't think about the consequences. After it went viral, she was barraged with hateful comments, questioning her story's validity. "You're too Black to be white," or "take your DNA," were some of the comments she received.

Regardless of the doubters and haters, Verda had documented proof of her racial journey, which she published in her autobiography, *Seventy Years of Blackness*.[54]

*   *   *

I didn't learn about Verda Byrd and her incredible story until seven years after it made national news. My racial story was just emerging, and I was immersed in writing *White Like Her*.

It was Dr. Margena Christian, former editor at *Ebony* and *Jet* magazines, senior lecturer at the University of Illinois at Chicago (UIC), and author of *It's No Wonder: The Life and Music of Motown's Sylvia Moy*, who brought Verda's story to my attention.

Margena and I became friends when I gave a campus lecture on *White Like Her* at UIC, where I earned an MA and PhD in English. Later, she asked me to be a guest lecturer in the class she was teaching.

When I told Margena I was looking for stories of family secrets and hidden identities, she suggested Verda Byrd. In Margena's substantial experience writing about race, she found that her articles about misattributed racial identities were the ones that sparked the most discussion, which comes as no surprise to me. In our highly charged racial environment, deciphering another's race has far reaching life-and-death consequences. As Josphine stated in Chapter 10, it goes back to belonging to a tribe.

In the case of mixed-race people whose physical appearances might not racially identify them, we're both fascinated and uneasy. And for people whose racial identities have been hidden from them, who've been lied to by their families, the discovery of their true identity is nothing short of traumatic.

As our Zoom interview begins, there's an immediate ease between us, as if we've known each other for years. Maybe it's the intersection of our racial discovery stories. Or maybe it's Verda. Friendly and engaging, she doesn't hold back. She's eager to share her story once again, even though, like me, she's experienced backlash from strangers.

Her white hair is loosely piled atop her head. She wears a sleeveless black-and-white patterned blouse open at the neck. Her skin is as white as mine.

But it's her long, rhinestone encrusted fingernails that catch my eye. They're as emphatic and singular as she is.

Verda begins her narrative with the adoption document that whiplashed her life. In 2013, cleaning out her personal papers, trying to downsize for a move, she came across an adoption paper with the name Jeanette Beagle. She'd seen the paper thirty-five years earlier when her adoptive mother, Edwinna Wagner, died. But because she and her husband, who was in the military, were overseas, she put it away and forgot about it.

"I saw the name Jeanette Beagle. But I had no idea who Jeanette Beagle was," Verda explains.

The adoption paper had no birth date. Rather than file the paper away, as she'd done in the past, she decided to find out who this person was.

Although Verda had known she was adopted since she was twelve years old, she never gave much thought to being adopted.

"At the age of twelve, my mind was not developed enough to know what adoption really meant. My mom said, 'You're adopted.' And I said, 'Okay.' That was it. And it never came up after that."

But now, puzzling over this adoption paper for Jeanette Beagle, she started questioning why her adopted mom never told her her birth name, her birth date, or her race. There was no one in her family to ask. All the aunts and uncles she'd known were dead. There was no one who could tell her who Jeanette Beagle was.

Verda says that was hard, but it wasn't the issue. The issue was wanting to know what really happened to her before she was adopted.

The Search for Jeanette Beagle

Verda's efforts to find out information about Jeanette Beagle immediately hit a roadblock that many adoptees encounter when looking for their birth parents: Her adoption records were sealed.

In 1946, when Verda's adoption took place, most adoptions in the United States were closed. As mentioned in an earlier chapter, the rationale behind sealing the records was in part to erase the stigma of illegitimacy associated with children born out of wedlock. Additionally, the states were protecting not only the birth parent or parents, but the adoptive parents from the social scorn of sterility.[55]

When Verda wrote to the Kansas City Juvenile Division in Missouri, where the adoption took place, she was denied access to her adoption records. The responding letter stated that they couldn't give her any information about Jeanette Beagle's adoption unless she went through a research person. The letter included a list of researchers. Verda contacted one who agreed to take on her case.

Because Missouri was a closed adoption state (and still is) the researcher had to verify that Verda's birth and adoptive parents were deceased or gave their consent to unseal the adoption records. This was to protect the confidentiality of the birth parents, with no regard to the adoptee's right to know their genetic identity. The researcher was able to prove to the Kansas City court that Verda's adoptive parents were dead, and she was granted access to the adoption documents.

Three months later, Verda received her original adoption document packet.

"I wasn't nervous," she says. "*What can they tell me that I don't already know?* is what I thought."

But she was wrong. Not only was she herself the Jeanette Beagle referenced on the birth certificate, but she was white. On some of the papers, both of her biological parents were listed as white.

"I read those papers over and over. I thought they must have sent me the wrong papers. Maybe they had the wrong address. Is this true? Maybe I'm not reading them right. I had not known this all my life. I had not known that I was white. My mind got stuck on being white. I couldn't get past that word. I lived seventy years as a Black woman. Now I was a white woman."

Her shock was so extreme, she considered shredding the papers. But because she considers adoption a major influence in one's life, she didn't shred them.

After two weeks of reading those same words over and over again, she began to try and make peace with her new racial identity.

"After I accepted the word white,"—Verda taps the desk and spells out "white"—"after I mentally accepted that, I said, 'What the hell. I'm not changing and going backwards. I'm seventy, I can't be reborn again.'"

Verda's use of "reborn" strikes at the intent behind sealed adoptions, which was to erase the adoptee's birth identity and replace it with the adopted identity.

"When the adoption takes place, the state issues a new birth certificate pronouncing the adoptee as born to the adoptive parents."[56]

Two years later, when she received her original birth certificate, which listed her birth parents as white, her race once again was verified as white.

Verda now had two birth certificates—in essence, two identities. Her original birth certificate declared her race as white. And the adoption birth certificate, which altered her race, said she was "Negro."

"I have two birth certificates. I've yet to understand how two women can carry the same baby for nine months," Verda says.

What Verda is sarcastically referring to is the Health Department's reissuing of her birth certificate in the name of Verda Ann Wagner. The new birth certificate names her father as Ray Wagner and her mother as Edwinna Wagner. Both are designated "Negro." But most disturbing for Verda is that it falsely claims that Edwinna was the biological mother. Section 7 asks the number of months of pregnancy. The number written in the space was "9."

For the majority of Verda's life, this reissued document would be her official birth certificate for school and for all legal and government matters.

The packet also contained documents, such as her parent's petition to adopt her and personal correspondence between social workers and Edwinna Wagner. These documents provided Verda with a window into her early life, which she has no memory of. And, most importantly, they explained why she'd been relinquished by her mother—a question that every adoptee wants answered.

Jeanette Beagle's Short Life

Verda was born Jeanette Marie Beagle on September 27, 1942, to Daisy and Earl Beagle, a white couple living in Kansas City, Missouri. She was their fifth child. Around the time of Jeanette's birth, Earl joined the Army and, in effect, deserted the family.

Left to raise five children, Daisy was looking for work in Kansas City, Missouri, when she fell thirty feet from a train trestle and was struck by a street car, sustaining multiple internal injuries. Due to the extent and seriousness of Daisy's injuries, she was confined to the hospital for a year. During that time, her five children were placed in a children's home under the auspices of the welfare system.

After being released from the hospital, Daisy was faced with a difficult decision regarding her five children. Unable to find Earl and financially strapped, she decided it would be best to allow her fourth child, and the baby, Jeanette, to remain in the children's home, mainly because they were still in diapers. She took the other three children home with her.[57]

Wanting clarification of what a children's home was, I ask Verda to explain.

"It was where unwed mothers would put their babies. 'Children's home' was the other name for the welfare system."

According to the foster care requirements, Jeanette had to remain in the welfare system for one year before she was even eligible to be placed in a foster home or be adopted.

After a year in foster care, Jeanette was placed with Ray and Edwinna Wagner, an affluent, childless Black couple from Newton, Kansas. They took Jeanette into their home as a foster child.

The Wagners offered Jeanette a stable and secure life. Ray Wagner was a train porter for the Santa Fe Railroad, owned his own house, and made a comfortable living. He would later be part of a discriminatory lawsuit against the railroad company. Edwinna was a stay-at-home wife, but also had worked as a stenographer.

In January 1944, when Jeanette was two years old, Daisy signed consent to adopt papers releasing Jeanette to the state of Missouri. Earl couldn't sign the papers until he was discharged from the Army, so he signed the same papers in 1945.

The Wagners applied to adopt Jeanette in early 1946. Before they were approved, the Kansas Children's Home and Service League conducted a thorough study of the Wagners' home.

In her autobiography, Verda includes the adoption acceptance letter from the children's home dated October 7, 1946. The letter lists the child's name as JEANETTE BEAGLE. However, at the bottom of the letter it states, "Petitioners request . . . that the name of said child be changed to VERDA ANN WAGNER."[58]

Not only was Jeanette's name changed, but the state approved a transracial adoption by placing a white child with a Black family. At the time, it was considered transgressive for a Black couple to adopt a white child.[59] According to Verda, she was the first known transracial adoption.

Even though the state was well aware that Jeanette's original birth certificate listed her parents as white, it's not clear if in approving her adoption by a Black couple they ignored her race or if they determined Jeanette was a "light-skinned" Black child because a Black couple wanted to adopt her.

The documentation papers sent to Verda hint at how the state justified the adoption of a white child by a Black couple. However, they don't fully explain the why.

In a letter sent by Kansas Children's Home and Service League to the Adoption Department's Juvenile Court in Missouri regarding the Wagners' fitness to adopt Jeanette, the social worker felt that "either a rather light child or a dark brown, rather than black coloring, would fit best in this home."[60]

The letter seems to infer that Jeanette is not white, despite her birth certificate, and that she would be a good fit for the Wagners. While Ray and Edwinna were both designated "Negro" on documentation, it's evident from Edwinna's photographs that she's a light-skinned Black woman. Hence, the social worker's statement about a light child or a dark brown child. Was the state using the practice of matching to justify Verda's adoption?

Since so much time has passed and all the parties involved are deceased, it's impossible to know the motives of the officials involved in Jeanette's adoption.

However, what is beyond dispute is Jeanette's genetic heritage and identity were erased by the state. Not until Verda investigated her adoption, did she realize her true racial heritage.

Another letter written by Edwinna to the social worker casts light on the trauma Verda experienced after the adoption. While Edwinna stresses that Verda was adjusting well, the letter hints otherwise:

> She is doing fine, having had only two periods (sic) of homesickness where she cried to go back to her other mama and daddy (sic), and wanted her other play things. But we are hoping she will forget in time, although she has such a wonderful memory, in fact, we have found her to have a brilliant mind in comparison to a child of five or six.[61]

During our second interview, I ask Verda who her "other mama and daddy" were.

She says, "I was too young to remember. But there were women in the children's home who took care of us. Maybe that's who I called 'mama.'"

When I tell her about other adoptees that I interviewed and the trauma they suffered when they discovered they were adopted, she smiles, and says, "As an adoptee, I can't speak for everyone. But for me, I'm not a victim of nothing. I'm a survivor."

Monday and Tuesday Are My White Days; The Rest Are My Black Days

Verda grew up in the predominantly white town of Newton, Kansas, home of the Mennonite school, Bethel College. Because the town was small, the schools were integrated. There were about eight to ten Black families. In high school, Verda's friends were white.

"I never experienced racism. My skin was lighter. My high school friends and their parents never saw my adoptive parents. That's why in Newton, I never experienced racism," she explains.

Although she never questioned that she was Black, she remembers an incident that hinted at her racial heritage.

"After taking my driver's license test at sixteen, I received my license in the mail. It said 'W' for 'white.' I showed it to my mom, and she said, 'Oh, they made a mistake.' Newton people thought I was white to begin with."

Regardless of what the outside world thought Verda's race was, she considered herself Black. At twenty-one, when she moved to St. Paul, Minnesota, for a job, she became even more immersed in Black culture.

"I began to have Black boyfriends, go to Black churches, and go to Black social clubs."[62]

In 1968, she moved to Colorado and married Kenneth Johnson, a light-skinned Black man. After they divorced, nine years later she married another Black man, Trancle Byrd, in 1979, who served in the Air Force. As a military spouse, Verda and her husband traveled the world.

Even though she was light-skinned, she listed her race as "Black" on all official documents.

"I always put 'Black.' Nobody said anything to me because during the sixties, seventies, and eighties, if you were Black, you were Black. No questions asked. When I dated, I dated Black men. I didn't know I was white," Verda says.

"Now that you know about your racial heritage," I ask, "how do you identify yourself on documents or health forms?"

The question that goes to the heart of race and racial identity. The question I'm constantly asked.

"I just had to fill out a health form for a new doctor. And there was this race box. I checked 'Other.' Because 'Other' covers both races. If you want to know what 'Other' means, ask me," she answers.

"Does that mean you think of yourself as mixed race?"

I gently push her for a more definitive answer. My interest isn't in proving or disproving that Earl Beagle was Verda's birth father. My interest is in how Verda views herself racially after her discovery of white parents and the subsequent public backlash.

"Monday and Tuesday are my white days. Because it's the beginning of the week. It was the beginning of my life. I was white. The first forty-eight hours of the week is all I can give my whiteness. The rest of the days of the week, and the rest of my life have been Black. So, today being Friday, today is my Black day."

Although I appreciate her clever response, she hasn't definitively answered my question. Does her hesitation come from the online attacks and news articles that doubted Earl Beagle was her birth father?

I sympathize with Verda's hesitation, having had my share of online attacks and nasty emails. However, my attackers' motives focused on some bizarre notion that I was after money and/or reparations.

Other than my first public encounter during a library talk, where an audience member rudely grilled me on my identity and asked "What are you anyway?" no one has ever questioned that my mother was passing as white. Maybe because why would I, a seemingly white woman, admit to Black heritage in this racially charged culture if it wasn't true? I've also publicly shared my DNA from two separate tests, one of which was conducted by PBS's *Genealogy Roadshow*.

While Verda told me in our first interview that she'd had two DNA tests, she was vague about their results. So, I ask her again.

"Are you willing to share your DNA results?" I probe, trying to determine if DNA figures into her sense of self. It certainly figured into mine: 7–9 percent African heritage, depending on the test.

When she answers I can almost feel her bristle.

"No," she says with conviction. "I'm not going to tell you or anybody else what those tests say. I think that's a personal thing."

Then she elaborates. "DNA does not make a person your mama. Love makes a family. DNA tells you what race you are, what culture you're supposed to be from. That's what DNA does. It doesn't tell me that you got to be my sister. It doesn't say that."

Now I think I understand her clever answer about white days and Black days. She's decided that culture trumps DNA. It doesn't matter what a DNA test says.

It's her message to the haters who've attacked her:

"I decide who I am. Not you."

As to Earl Beagle being her biological father, Verda says, "I accept that Earl is my birth father. I don't have any other documentation that says he isn't."

She admits that Daisy and Earl had issues, but she lauds them for their decision to relinquish her for adoption.

"Both knew they could give me a better life by putting me up for adoption. They said Earl was going and coming, going and coming. He was possibly an alcoholic. I read and heard that Daisy had Black men. That I'm too Black to be white. I don't care about the issues they had. The issue they agreed on was for me, child number five, to have a better life."

Verda comes back to being a survivor: "What other people think about whether Daisy and Earl were my parents, they can think anything they want to. I have the documentation. I had no idea how far my story would go; what the circumstances or consequences would be; but the good lord only gives us as much as we can bear. Seems like it's hard, but we'll get through it."

More Than a Survivor

Verda has more than survived, she's flourished. Using her celebrity, in 2020, she founded the Seventy Years of Blackness Scholarship Fund. The fund provides partial or full scholarships for young people "aging out" of the foster system who are seeking trade school certification. She's also an advocate for transracial adoption. Verda says that helping others has helped her cope with her PTSD, which she still experiences as a result of her unexpected racial discovery.

Her documentary, *Seventy Years of Blackness: The Untangling of Race and Adoption*, won eight documentary film awards and multiple nominations.

Verda ends our interview with a quip from her husband, Trancle, who, when he learned of Verda's biological parents, said, "I went to bed with a Black woman, and woke up with a white woman."

Then she laughs and says, "Don't forget today's Friday. It's my Black day."

CHAPTER 15

The Reluctant Seeker

Jack Rocco, MD: Mt. Gilead, North Carolina

ADOPTEE JACK ROCCO NEVER HAD ANY INTEREST IN FINDING HIS BIRTH parents. Why would he? As the oldest male child in a close-knit Italian family, he was treated like a prince. He was the favorite.

Then a random blind date changed his mind. What he discovered about his birth parents and the secret his adoptive parents had kept from him upended his life. When Jack finally confronted his adoptive father with the truth of his identity, his father replied, "Five people went to their graves with that secret. We were trying to protect you."

* * *

Jack Rocco exudes a quiet, reassuring confidence that he must have honed during his rigorous medical training and his years of experience as an orthopedic surgeon. His affable, easy-going manner draws me in. I feel I can ask him anything; tell him anything.

His physical appearance tells me nothing about his ethnicity or race.

Like Bruce-Paul Scott from Chapter 9, whose mixed-race identity was hidden from him, Jack's head is shaved. And like Bruce, growing up, Jack's friends teased him about his dark, kinky hair calling it a "Brillo pad." But it never occurred to Jack that he was anything but what his adoptive parents told him—Italian, German, and Irish.

Fellow adoptee Brad Ewell referred me to Jack. Brad had appeared on Jack's podcast: *Our Best Interests: Adopted – Life Lessons from Childhood Trauma to Adulthood*. Jack co-hosts the podcast with fellow adoptee, Michael Rocco (no relation).

Before I ask him a question, he begins talking about his forthcoming memoir, *Recycled: A Reluctant Search for True Self Through Nurture, Nature, and Free Will*. (The book was published in 2023.) He says he originally wrote the book for himself, not for publication.

"Though it was finished about a year and a half ago, I didn't really want to come out with it, because of my parents. It was more done for me. I was thinking they might be sensitive to it because they were integral to it," Jack says.

The fear of offending the adoptive parents runs deep in some adoptees—sometimes deeper than the need to find their birth parents.

However, Jack eventually changed his mind and published the book. He cites several reasons.

"My parents are getting older and are having some health issues. I really wanted them to understand my underlying appreciation for everything they did. I feel myself far on the spectrum of blessed or lucky adoptees."

He broke the news of the book two weeks prior to our conversation.

"I went up to visit and told them. I thought they were going to be defensive and resistant to it."

But they weren't, perhaps because Jack and his adoptive parents had been down this road before, four years earlier.

After Jack explained the book was about his adoption story and reassured them that he included his grandma and her raviolis, his father said, "Jack, that's going to be a great book. I want Sylvester Stallone to play me."

Then he says something that surprises me.

"I appreciate the lies and the truth because I benefitted from them both."

None of the adoptees I interviewed ever said they appreciated the lies. They felt the lies contributed to their trauma and sense of betrayal.

Not until I hear Jack's story will I understand what he means.

It Was Like I Was a Dirt Bag

Orthopedic surgeon; former captain in the U.S. Air Force; one of the founders of One Step (OSS), an organization providing free health care to orphans in Madagascar; author; and podcaster—from the outside, Jack Rocco's life epitomizes success.

Yet, if you peel back the layers, he'll tell you that he attributes some of his success to overcompensating for his insecurities as an adoptee.

"I wanted to be the ultimate Italian. The ultimate medical student, doctor, father, and husband," he says.

Jack's nurturing and supportive upbringing in a close-knit, working-class Italian American family also contributed to his success. Born and raised in Erie, Pennsylvania, he was the oldest son of the oldest son. He describes himself as "the prince." No one ever made an issue of his being adopted. No one ever said he didn't belong.

The story he was told by his adoptive parents about his birth parents was that they were two young college kids who couldn't afford to raise a baby. They put him up for adoption so he could have a better life.

"They said my father was Italian and my mother was German and Irish, which is the exact ethnicity of my adopted parents. I never really thought that was strange. I never questioned what I was."

However, he does remember fantasizing about his birth parents.

"When I was probably five or six, any time we were in public, I remember looking at other weird-looking kids. Looking for others like

me, and dreaming and thinking I was going to run into my parents
or an adopted sibling. Apparently, I had some insecurities about my
appearance."

What Jack was doing was looking for someone in the crowd who
looked like him, a genetic mirror of himself, a search for his tribe.[63]

Regardless of his insecurities, or maybe because of them, Jack was
an overachiever both academically and in sports.

After graduating from the University of Pittsburgh, he attended the
Temple University School of Medicine, followed by a rigorous orthopedic surgical residency at Temple. It was during his residency that Jack's
world was turned upside down by a random blind date. During dinner,
Jack asked his date about her parents. When the woman said that she
was adopted, Jack told her he was adopted.

"I asked her if she wanted to find her real parents, because everyone always asked me that. She said, 'Actually, I did find my parents.'
And that kinda of shocked me. I totally believed that it couldn't be
done. My adoption records were locked by the courts. It was illegal to
do it."

Jack makes the gesture for quotation marks when he says "illegal."

His date said that she'd been told that her birth parents were two
young college kids who couldn't raise a baby. However, as it turned
out, it wasn't true. Her mother was an alcoholic, who'd had a rough
life.

"I told her that was my exact same story. She said that it probably wasn't true. And that the nuns told everyone the same story. That
was the first chink in my armor, where my belief system was first challenged," Jack says.

The woman must have seen that Jack was reeling, trying to digest
her cynical comment about the false adoption stories. She suggested
they go to a bookstore after dinner where he could buy Betty Jean Lifton's book, *The Journey of the Adopted Self.*

Jack spent the entire next day reading the book.

"It was as if the book was written for me. All these issues with adoptees, their insecurities, even their hypervigilance. I was like, holy shit, this is speaking to me."

He was supposed to go to a dinner that night for the entire orthopedic department. As one of the honored residents, he was expected to be there. He called and said he was too sick to attend.

"I was knocked for a loop. You talk about your loss of identity. We believe our parents and we believe the authorities. The Catholic church wouldn't lie. It crushed me. I remember telling a friend it was like I was a dirt bag. I knew nothing. It was the loss of my story. I believe that so much of our identity is tied to our story."

Jack's deep dive into adoption didn't stop with Lifton's book. His extensive reading introduced him to the idea that his separation from his mother after his birth caused a trauma.

"I'm a full-fledged believer in separation trauma. It's a disturbance that does change the neural development. Though I'm not an expert in this."

Jack says, "To me, it makes sense logically. If a child is suddenly abandoned, I think they do have a hyper-alertness. To my knowledge, I had probably fifteen minutes with my birth mother. And that was it. Then six weeks in an orphanage before my parents adopted me."

Left wondering what the real story was about his birth parents, Jack decided to do what he calls "a little bit of a seek." For a brief period, he submitted his name to an adoption registry site. About two weeks later, a yellow sticky note was left on his desk at work. It said, DR. R., AMY CALLED. SHE SAYS SHE'S AN OLD FRIEND. GIVE HER A CALL.

Jack didn't have any old friends in Philadelphia, so immediately his imagination went into hyperdrive. Questions and hopes were zinging around in his head.

"Oh, my God, it's my birth mother. She saw the registry. She found me at work. How did she know I worked here? Maybe she follows me. Maybe she's known all along."

He called the number and got an answering machine.

"I listened to it. She sounded just like me. I can tell by her voice that she has long black Italian hair. I was so nervous I hung up."

He's not sure how many times he called and hung up. Eventually, a woman answered.

"Hi, this is Jack. You called me," he said.

"Who?' she asked.

"I got a message someone was looking for Dr. R. in the orthopedic office."

"Oh, that was me," she replied. "But I was looking for Dr. Resnick. They must have given the message to the wrong Dr. R."

Taken aback with both disappointment and relief, Jack says, "It was a busy part of my life. I didn't have time for all that emotion."

The mistaken encounter ended Jack's search for his birth parents. He was done. Or at least he thought he was.

Suddenly, My Entire Story Had Been Blown Up

Jack married in 2004, and soon after they were expecting their first child. During his wife's pregnancy, she asked him if he wanted to know his medical history, in case the child wanted to know.

Initially, he resisted, but his wife was persistent.

"If I get the paperwork and fill it out, will you sign it?"

Reluctantly, he agreed, convinced nothing would come of it.

"At that point in my life, I didn't even believe I was adopted anymore. That's how much of the Kool-Aid I drank. I almost believed my parents were lying to me." He pauses. "But I also knew it was true. I was adopted. I did always feel different from my adoptive parents."

Three years after submitting the paperwork, Jack received a call from a representative from the state concerning his adoption. The woman explained that they'd just picked up his file and had some leads. She would let him know if anything came of it. Jack was secretly hoping it wouldn't work out.

Three days later, the representative called and said that they'd found his mother and had talked to her.

"The woman said, 'Here's her name, her email, and phone number. She sounds very cool. Give her a call. And there's something else: One of your parents is African American.'"

"I just wasn't surprised," Jack says. "I guess I was in too much shock that I found my mother because I felt that my subconscious mind knew that."

Jack went home and googled his mother, who had a webpage. When he saw her photo, he said, "Those are my eyes."

Other than seeing himself in his daughter, this was only the second time in Jack's life that he'd experienced genetic mirroring. He also discovered that his mother's family came on the Mayflower.

"I say in the first chapter of my book that if you're Italian in Erie, PA, you're automatically Catholic, a democrat, a Yankees fan, and then American. As far as your identity goes, that's pretty inclusive—ethnicity, country of origin, political affiliation, religious beliefs, and sports teams. So within an hour, I've got this English settler of privilege. Then, oh yeah, the other parent is African American and came on a slave ship from Africa." He's smiling and laughing at the irony.[64]

"Suddenly, my entire story had been blown up." When he says this, I see a sadness in his eyes. His Italian American identity was gone.

The next day he called his birth mother.

A Black Farmer Named Larry

"Hello, Jack, I was waiting to hear from you," were Jack's birth mother's first words to him. His birth mother said she'd thought of him often, but knew he had to be the one to make contact. They clicked instantly.[65]

Contrary to what Jack's random blind date told him years ago about the nuns telling all adoptive parents that the birth parents were young college students, his birth parents in fact were two young college students.

Jack says that his birth mother barely knew his father.

"They'd had a brief relationship. After a doctor confirmed the pregnancy, she walked to the college football field where my birth father was practicing football and told him. What he said, I'm not sure. But it was obvious they weren't marrying. And she wasn't going to keep the child on her own. She didn't want to be a single parent."

Jack relates the details of his birth mother's pregnancy and his birth with painful precision.

"She did what all the women did back then. She went to the maternity home, had me, signed me away, then she came back home as if nothing happened. She 'didn't have a choice.' Her parents weren't too happy. She clearly went through a lot of emotions."

Jack learned that his birth father's name was Larry. He remembered his parents telling him that the nuns had called him Larry. All this time, they thought the nuns had made up the name, when in fact it was his birth father's name.

His birth mother emailed Jack two photos of Larry. He was amazed at how much he looked like him. To prove his point, he shows me one of the photos of his birth father in college. They have the same distinctive chin and eyebrows.

According to his birth mother, Larry had a darker complexion, but was very light skinned. She wasn't sure of his race. Although the state representative said one of his parents was African American, not until Jack received the 1966 court documents, did he see his racial designation: "Negro child."

"*Was I really Black?*" Jack asked himself. And what did that mean?

She also told him that his birth father had died about a year ago, nixing any possibility of meeting him.

"I brooded on the information. In retrospect, I probably should have had counseling. I should have had some resources to help me through that. I didn't have anything."

Jack and his birth mother continued emailing for several months before meeting in person. He states that there was an ease to their conversations that only two people with the same shared secret could have.

His wife was supportive and even joked when he told her about his father's race. In his book, *Recycled*, he quotes her as saying, "I thought I was marrying a white doctor named Jack. It turns out I married a Black farmer named Larry."[66] (At the time they were living on an old farm.)

Eventually Jack's wife and two children met his birth mother. He introduced her to his children as "one of daddy's friends," fearful his young son might tell his adoptive parents about having another grandmother. He wasn't ready to tell his parents yet. Although Jack did tell his sister, who also was adopted, about his birth mother and swore her to secrecy.

He laughs that he and his birth mother were like clandestine lovers. She was the other woman. When his son was a little older, he told both children that "daddy's friend" was really their grandmother. His daughter said that she figured that's who she was.

But Jack admits that meeting his birth mother and learning about his birth father did mess with him, and in some part contributed to his marital issues.

"We never had good communication to begin with. My parentage wasn't something we could talk about. And I was way too busy with my career."

Jack and his wife separated in 2017. At that time, he moved south for a new position; and his wife moved north with the children, plunging him into a depression.

"I always sensed this adoption thing is still messing with me. That's why less than six months after moving to North Carolina, I decided I needed to find my father's family," he explains. "Something deeper was eating at me. I was trying to understand what this sense of blackness is that I'm reported to have."

Man, You're the Spitting Image

With the help of his birth mother, Jack found a cousin on his father's side who lives ninety minutes from him in Fayetteville, North Carolina.

After connecting with his father's cousin, Jack found out that he had four half-siblings living within three hours of him. Serendipitously, his birth father had moved to Wilmington, North Carolina, years ago.

His cousin showed Jack a photo of Larry and his six brothers, relaying that possibly two of his father's brothers passed for white throughout their lives. One brother's wife didn't know he was Black until after he died, when his Black family showed up at the funeral. Of the seven brothers, only one was still living.

Over the next month or so, Jack met two other cousins and his birth father's only surviving brother.

When his uncle saw him, he said, "Man, you're the spitting image."

Jack describes his uncle as "a cool sixties dude with a black flat cap and leather jacket."

Eventually, at a potluck dinner, he met his four half-siblings, one of whom was five months younger than him. They had no knowledge of his existence. During the dinner, his half-siblings and their mother told him about Larry's life.

His father had served in Vietnam. When he returned, he completed his degree in special education and worked as a teacher for years. Reportedly, he was passed over for an administrative role. Frustrated, he left teaching entirely. It wasn't clear when, but at some point, he abandoned his family and started driving a limo in Atlantic City, New Jersey, where he died from alcoholism.

In trying to understand his birth father's choices, Jack says there are many missing links. However, he views his father's life as a mixed-race man within its historical context. He was told that his father was too white for Black people, and too Black for white people.

"I had to look into what it was like to be a Black man who was mixed in the sixties when life was so divided. Was he Black? Was he white? When he returned from Vietnam, he was trying to assimilate in a white world. I think he was trying to pass, though my birth mother wasn't sure. I've come to the conclusion that he wasn't a bad guy."

For Jack, the question of his "new" identity troubles him.

"I haven't taken a DNA test because I don't know who's going to be using it." Then he adds, "Putting your identity back together is knowing what this unknown race/ethnicity is about."

Knowing what it's about, not just what it is, I think, having experienced the same dilemma of racial confusion. Held in the dark of your deepest self, raised without exposure to a part of your identity, messes with your sense of who you are, who you can be, and where you fit in the world.

Jack felt there was only one more thing he needed to do—share with his adoptive parents the journey he'd been on since finding his birth mother eleven years ago. It was time to end the secrecy.

Five People Went to Their Graves with That Secret

On Father's Day weekend 2018, Jack decided to tell his adoptive parents that he'd established a relationship with his birth mother and had met his birth father's family. But before he did, he told his sister what he planned to do.

She cautioned him not to do it.

"They're too old. They don't want to know."

He assured her that it would be fine. He couldn't have been more wrong.

"I told them that I'd found my birth parents and siblings. But I didn't say anything about race. Even though I reassured them that finding my birth mother and my birth father's family only made me appreciate them more, when I finished, everyone was crying. My father was red-faced and shaking.

"'Jack, five people went to their graves with that secret.'"

Jack wasn't sure what secret he was referring to. Was it that he was mixed race? So, he asked.

"You mean that my father was Black?"

"Yes."[67]

Two days later, his mother called Jack and said his father wanted everything to go back to how it was. And that's exactly what they did. They didn't talk about it for four years.

*   *   *

During the COVID lockdown, Jack decided to write a memoir about his adoption and everything changed for him yet again.

Writing the book, *Recycled*, was cathartic for him and was never meant for publication. It was written for himself, his children, and anyone else interested in his story. He tells me that writing it has helped him speak to me about his adoption story.

I fully understand what he means. Writing *White Like Her* allowed me to talk about race and racial discrimination in an authentic way, even though I'd rarely experienced racial discrimination. I feel I'm a bridge between my white heritage and my Black heritage, with a foot in each camp. And because of my ultra-white appearance, unless I reveal that I'm mixed race, no one knows my real identity.

For more than a year, Jack sat on the book, embarrassed. When he finally submitted it for publication and it was accepted, he told his adoptive parents, expecting them not to be pleased. But they surprised him.

After reading the book, they were excited for him. "Speaking with my parents recently, they were much more open to talking about my adoption."

While Jack doesn't blame or judge them for not telling him he was mixed race, he does question their reasons.

"Their story is, they didn't look at me as Black or mixed race or whatever. They looked at me as one of the family like everyone else," he explains. "Also, they thought if I knew I was mixed race, it would affect me in some negative fashion. Early on, it was the risk of discrimination. Later in life, it was like why mess with him, he's doing so well. Then at some point, I think they just forgot it was a lie," Jack explains.

"We start to believe these lies and get away with them for so long that we start to adopt the story as the truth. And then it gets too complicated to correct the web, so we sit in it and hope no one finds out. We all go along with the story because it's easier than the truth. They were good assimilators, like me. I would be a hypocrite to criticize them."

Regardless of their reasons, Jack believes his adoptive parents should have told him the truth of his heritage. When he told his father that, his response was, "Jack, you never asked."

His father offered him a stack of documents about him that he'd kept in a closet, if he wanted them. Jack just repeated that he should have told him. And his father said again that he never asked.

"It's ridiculous." Jack shakes his head. "But their alibi is just that I never questioned, so they never had to tell me."

On multiple occasions since then, they still haven't budged from their belief that it was on Jack to ask about his racial heritage.

*　*　*

Like many adoptees who learn as adults that they're adopted and/or of a different racial heritage, Jack wonders what his life would have been like if he'd known he was mixed race.

"For me, it's just that lost life. What would my life had been if I'd known from birth or from age twenty? Who would I have married if I'd known my race? What occupation would I have pursued?"

As to his identity?

"There have been people who've said, 'What are you? Are you Italian?' Now that I know, I mess with them a little bit. 'What do you think I am?' They say Italian. I guess I still struggle with am I Black? Am I white?"

For Jack, the most difficult part of navigating his discovery is that he can't change the previous fifty years—when he didn't know.

CHAPTER 16

A Surrendering Mother's Story

Diana

DIANA NEVER HAD ANY GREAT DESIRE TO HAVE CHILDREN. MARRIAGE YES, maybe at thirty. Then at twenty-one, a semester away from graduating from college, she found herself pregnant and unmarried. It was 1965. Her options were limited.

She makes no excuses for her predicament.

"It was a pretty stupid thing to do. And a hell of a mess."

Diana's gut-wrenching experience exposes the societal scorn heaped on unwed mothers, the pain of surrendering one's baby, and the almost unsurmountable difficulty of finding a surrendered child.

*   *   *

In August 2023, when I email Diana the release form to sign for the book, she goes silent. Five days later, she phones me with her concerns. She's not the first interviewee to balk at signing the consent form. Faced with the reality of the book's publication and ceding the right to approve the copy can be an unnerving prospect for some interviewees.

What did I say?

Will loved ones be hurt by something I revealed?

Do I really want my intimate story out there?

I offer her what I offered some of the other interviewees—complete anonymity. I also tell her she doesn't have to answer my follow-up questions, if they're too painful for her, which I suspect they are because she never did answer them. Although the follow-up questions would have added depth to her story, they aren't crucial.

She takes me up on both offers. She seems okay with the compromise.

Relieved that I can tell the adoption story from a surrendering mother's point of view, I resend an amended release form, stating I won't use her real name. But the clause that waives the right to inspect or approve the finished product, including written copy, remains.

Several weeks go by. She doesn't respond. Although I think she's decided not to sign the form, I try one more time.

Finally, she emails me back.

Hi, Gail,

Sorry to be so evasive. You may use the interview with a different name. I just don't want to be hashing this all out again. It was put in the background long ago, and I am done with thinking about it. Thanks for your tolerant and thoughtful courtesy. You can even say in your book that I am done with it. :) I'll look for your book when it comes out. Thanks.

I'm touched by her bravery and her willingness to share a part of her life that, as she says, she's done with.

I think of all the mothers who surrendered their children. I think of that time period when being an unmarried pregnant woman meant having little to no options over one's body and one's destiny.

Diana's reluctance reenforces the weight of responsibility that falls hard on my shoulders, the responsibility of telling these stories with integrity—and how much I need and want to both honor the stories and be truthful.

Release form in hand, I start to write her story from the transcription. On the first page, I'm startled by a note I wrote to myself, highlighted in yellow.

December. Tomorrow my brother will die.

My personal life interrupting my professional life. The impossible task of unweaving one from the other.

A Very Disconnecting Experience

Diana has a sadness in her voice, a weariness that I ascribe to the wisdom of acceptance.

Behind her a window casts sunlight across her silver hair and strong features. Only the corner of her open computer is visible. She's chosen the town's history center for our interview, which seems emblematic of how she wants to present herself—a woman in her seventies who's still intellectually active and involved, making a difference in other peoples' lives and dispelling any preconceived notions about older women and their usefulness.

When she tells me that genealogy has been her avocation for thirty years, I'm not surprised. Nor am I surprised when she says she's the founder of the town's history center and has a large genealogy history website that she began in 1996. After all, isn't genealogy the search for family, the leafing out of family trees, the finding of lost family and their stories, and sometimes their secrets?

What does surprise me is the reason she gives for her devotion to genealogy.

"It was a particular time for me. My husband, like your father, was

an alcoholic. He committed suicide in 1990. Which was a very discon-
necting experience."

She devotes one sentence to what must have been an incredibly difficult incident. I'm accustomed and sensitive to the interviewee's need
to hold parts of themselves back. After all, I'm a stranger, writing a
book. Can I be trusted?

Because I don't want to shut her down, I don't pursue the reasons
for his suicide or how it affected her. We haven't even gotten to the hard
questions yet.

Then she adds, "A couple of years later, my father gave me some of
our genealogy he'd gotten from a cousin. I had new genealogy software,
so I just jumped in. I got back six to seven generations in this county. It
immediately triggered me into this community. A small town like this,
there's a lot of interrelationships. In 2002, I founded the history center,
which began in my barn. In 2012, it was moved to one of the oldest
buildings in town."

She swivels back and forth in her chair, looking off to the side as
she tells me about her 131-acre farm that she bought from her parents
forty years ago.

"It's a nice property. I don't even see neighbors."

There's no right or easy way to shift the interview to her experience
of surrendering her baby. I ask if she has other children.

"No," she says.

Then we begin to talk about one of the toughest times in Diana's
life.

It Was a Total Outrage to Him

As noted in the beginning of the chapter, Diana was twenty-one and
unwed when she discovered she was pregnant. A senior in college, she
was just starting her student teaching, which would be her last semester
before graduating in January.

"I had high school seniors and I started showing pretty soon. But I had wonderful support from the professor in charge of my student teaching and the teacher I was working with. But it was an awkward situation," she explains.

Diana was fortunate that she was allowed to complete her student teaching. Up until 1970, when Title IX was enacted into law, pregnant high school and college girls were required to withdraw immediately. Society demanded banishment of the pregnant girl, punishing her for straying outside societal mores.[68]

Although she had no intention of marrying the baby's father, a light-skinned African American, who was a student at the same college, she did inform him of the pregnancy right away.

"I would have had an abortion, but abortions weren't legal then." She pauses. "It was a pretty stupid thing to do, and what a mess."

Further complicating the situation, which Diana didn't find out until much later, her baby's father impregnated another girl during this time. The pregnant girl had already given up one child and didn't want to give up another. So, they married and had other children together.

While her college professors were supportive, her parents were less so. She didn't tell them she was pregnant until it was obvious. She describes her relationship with her parents as "not emotionally close." Her mother was more sympathetic to her situation than her father.

"It was a total outrage to him. It was a terribly shameful thing. The whole rest of his life, he was sarcastic about it. Every once in a while, he'd make a snarky remark."

"How did that make you feel?" I ask, wondering how she dealt with lifelong disdain from her own father, which must have felt like having an old wound opened over and over.

"I'm sorry he took it the way he did. But that was him, that was his generation, that was the way he was. I really didn't take it personally."

Then she throws up one hand as if shooing away an insect.

"I didn't like it. I just ignored it."

What else could she do but armor herself? Not take it personally. Ignore it. But at what cost?

I Didn't Have Any Other Options

On the cusp of graduating from college, unwed and pregnant, Diana was uncertain what she should do. Her doctor suggested she go to a Florence Crittenton Home where she could have the baby. The home would facilitate the adoption.

"So, it was your decision to go to the home?" I naively ask.

She corrects me.

"I didn't have any other options. The generation behind us doesn't understand how it was back then. You couldn't get birth control if you weren't married. And an illegal abortion wasn't a safe alternative. I didn't want to die in the process."

For many pregnant unwed mothers, maternity homes were the only option. By the 1950s, the Florence Crittenton Association of America, the Salvation Army, Catholic Charities, and other organizations operated more than two hundred maternity homes in forty-five states. Altogether, the homes could house about twenty-five thousand young women a year, and because of the proliferation of unwed mothers, they turned away thousands more.[69]

Diana explains that you didn't go to the maternity home until you were fairly far along in your pregnancy. You could only stay there for ten, maybe twelve weeks at the most. She went to a Florence Crittenton Home in March of 1966. She was due in May. The cost of her stay was about $300. Her father pressured the baby's father to pay for the maternity home. And he did.

"My parents took me there."

She bites her lip, as if holding back the painful memory.

"My mom visited me one time. Because she doesn't drive, she had to take a bus, which was quite an effort for her. It was across the state line, about a couple hundred miles away from where we lived."

I can't imagine her loneliness and her fear being left alone in this strange place with strangers to deliver her first child without any friends or family there to support her.

Diana describes the home as okay—a nice building, small staff, one woman in charge—which tells me nothing and everything. It's the way a person describes something they want to forget.

"We were three to a room. We were not allowed to use last names. So, just a lot of different stories. We had chores to do. Nothing major. Set the table, wash the dishes, sweep the steps," she says.

When she talks about the actual adoption, she becomes more forthcoming, explaining how little input she had about a decision that altered her life forever.

"There were so many babies up for adoption then that many of the adoption agencies were at the saturation point. Only one had capacity for me. And it was Catholic. Because I was non-religious at the time, I didn't like the idea of adopting to a Catholic family. But I wasn't in a position to make choices. I had to go with whomever could accommodate me," Diana explains.

"And the racial thing was a major issue at the time. It wasn't to me. Or even to my parents. The baby's father was a very light-skinned person. It wasn't that I expected any extreme differences from myself and the child. Wouldn't have mattered to me anyway. But to the adoption, it was a major thing. Because back then a mixed-race child was not as adoptable as another."

Later, she learned through reading and hearing other people's adoption stories that lighter-skinned, mixed-race babies were often placed with Italian families, which would be the case with her child.

She relates an adoption story that reveals her own fears for her child.

"I worked at Nabisco with a man who had one natural child and one adopted child. Though the adopted child was clearly Black, he would say he's not Black. This child was being brought up with people who deliberately denied who he was. I was wondering how this child could grow up with everybody denying who he was?"

Seeing her colleague deny his adopted son's Black identity troubled Diana. Had the people who adopted her son erased his mixed-race identity and replaced it with a white identity? If so, what impact would that have on his sense of self if he discovered his racial heritage?

Another request Diana made regarding her son's adoption was that she wanted him to be adopted by people with an education.

"I made that very clear to the social worker nun who handled my case."

None of her wishes were honored.

Never Really Sure I Did the Right Thing

Like any new mom, after her baby was born, she wanted to see him.

"When I saw him, I was laughing. He looked so much like his father. It just amused me. His skin tone was light. At the time, I didn't see anything of myself in him."

They brought him to her a couple of times after his birth.

When she asked to see him again, they told her that the social workers had already taken him.

It's unclear if that was true. The operating belief that governed maternity homes for unwed mothers was if the mother saw the infant too many times, she would bond and wouldn't want to relinquish the child. It was better if it was a clean break, a severing of ties, a forgetting.

Diana seems to echo that sentiment.

"I didn't want to spend a lot of time with him. I didn't want to enable any attachments that would make it more difficult. I had no second thoughts. I had no vision of moving forward."

After her child's birth, she had no further contact with the baby's father. A few years later, she married. Although her parents and her husband's parents put pressure on her to have children, she didn't succumb to their pressure. She didn't want any more children.

"It was emotionally traumatic giving up a child. It's a grief like any other loss. You're never really sure that you did the right thing. You just hope that you did."

Diana seems agitated, almost defensive. Without question, surrendering her child traumatized her. Could the trauma have been so great that the thought of having another child was unbearable for her?

Even though Diana surrendered her child, she didn't forget him.

"I always hoped at some point that I would meet him. As time went on and I started to get into my sixties, I became concerned that might never happen."

Legally, to Live as Strangers Forever

To legally certify the adoption, Diana had to sign papers that she wouldn't try and find him. There's an edge to her voice as she describes her feelings about signing the papers.

"Legally, to live as strangers forever."

Despite signing the papers, she did log on to a couple of online forums for adopted people and looked at a few people who were born on the same date and at the same place. But nothing came of that. She also felt that it should be her son's decision to make contact with her. So, she waited and hoped.

Finally, one day, her hopes were fulfilled. She was contacted through the Orphans' Court in the county. It was her son's wife, who had prompted him to find his birth mother. She was pregnant and wanted to know what she was dealing with medically. When he dragged his heels filling out the paperwork, she filled out the forms.

Unfortunately, his request sat there for two and a half years.

When the Orphans' Court finally contacted Diana, they sent her a letter. She called them immediately, and said it was okay to make contact. The next day he called.

"I was nervous when I first talked to him. I didn't want to say the wrong thing. But I guess it doesn't matter what you say. In a way, it's going to be the wrong thing. You know nothing about this person. I just wanted to be sure he knew that I wanted to be in contact with him. And I wanted to know that he was healthy and had gotten a good education, and had a good life."

He assured her that he had a great life. He'd received a wonderful education, had two children, and a job he loved. His life was purposeful and meaningful.

Although her son had received an excellent education, several of her other fears for him were realized. He was never told that his birth father was African American, and he was raised in the Catholic religion. As Diana suspected, his adoptive parents were Italian, and he'd never been told he was mixed race.

"He was raised Italian. He loved being Italian. He was thoroughly engrossed in the culture. So, I think it's more a loss of being Italian than the racial thing. He's just baffled," Diana explains. "I think it was overpowering for him at first."

She also explained to him why she'd surrendered him for adoption, which he seemed to accept.

Initially, he didn't tell his adoptive parents that he'd found his birth mother. When his sister was diagnosed with a disease, he'd suggested to them that they find his sister's birth parents. Seeing their negative response convinced him to remain silent about his own discovery.

Although he arranged for Diana to visit him, his wife, and his children once a year, he didn't tell his children who Diana was to him until recently.

"There was no place in their life for me," Diana says. "I was an old woman who came to visit once a year. I didn't fit in any place. It was very sad to me that he had to hide this from his parents."

Eventually, Diana's son did tell his adoptive parents about her, and it was a disaster.

"I'm not exactly sure why, but it was a hysterical episode for the whole family. So, they just left it." Diana says.

But with time, his adoptive parents have come to terms with him finding his birth mother. However, Diana is still not included in any of their family events.

As to her relationship with her son, she characterizes it as "friends."

"I'm still cautious. Because he's dealing with emotional things, I'm very careful not to step over any invisible lines that might be there."

And their relationship now?

"I leave it to him if he wants to make contact. If he emails me, I email back. If he calls, we talk. It's just all in his hands. I don't suggest to him what he should be doing. If he asks for help, I give it."

You Have to Live with Your Decisions

We circle back to that traumatic time in her life, unwed and pregnant, with little options.

"It was a transitional period when I got pregnant—finishing college, starting a career. I'm already in the middle of a transition and have to deal with the pregnancy, the birth, and afterwards. That, of course, is the point of trauma. I thought about him a lot and as time went on, I thought about him even more. There was less and less time for this reunion to happen."

She shrugs her shoulder.

"But from a legal point of view, I signed it all away. I was the decision-maker. You have to live with your decisions. Though, I was young and inexperienced. I've had students from the university who've worked here at the town's history center and it's just amazing the basic things they don't know. They don't know that they don't know."

PART III

Donor Conceived

Chapter 17

Resurrecting Ghost Fathers

A History of Secrecy and Deceit

FROM ITS ONSET, HUMAN ARTIFICIAL INSEMINATION BY DONOR (AID) WAS plagued by ethical, legal, and moral issues. Due to these issues, the procedure was steeped in secrecy, and in some cases, deception, making it especially difficult for donor-conceived people to find their biological fathers.

The first known AID in the US, performed in 1884 by American physician and medical school professor, Dr. William Pancoast, is an example of such a deception.

Dr. Pancoast, without the consent of an infertile couple he was treating, inseminated the wife under anesthesia with the sperm of a medical student. He stated that he chose this particular person because he was good-looking. Hardly a criterion for choosing a sperm donor.

"The woman . . . gave birth nine months later and did not know that she had been impregnated with a donor's sperm. Her husband, whom Pancoast determined was infertile, later found out about the procedure from Pancoast."[70]

There's no record of the husband's reaction upon learning of the doctor's deceit. Did he feel the ends justified the means? After all, they had a healthy baby. Did he bow to the doctor's authority? We'll never know.

It's also impossible to know Dr. Pancoast's motives in not obtaining the couple's consent prior to the procedure, and in not telling the wife that the child was not her husband's. Not only did Pancoast breach the medical code of ethics in not obtaining the couple's permission for the procedure, he, conspiring with the husband, deceived the wife into thinking the child she bore and raised was her husband's. And, of course, the child would never know her true genetic identity.

Regardless of Pancoast's or the husband's motives, their actions were unethical. From our twenty-first century perspective, they might be considered criminal. Inseminating a non-consenting woman with a stranger's sperm could be viewed as medical rape.

As to the sperm donor, his identity remained secret. All the husband knew was that he was a handsome medical student.

In contrast to the first recorded AID in the United States, which shielded the names of the husband and wife, an equally well-known AID occurred in 1934, which revealed the names of the couple who willingly consented to the AID procedure.

News-Week published an article on this successful artificial insemination by donor titled: "'Ghost' Fathers: Children Provided for the Childless." I'm struck by the term "ghost fathers," which seems both apropos and prophetic. In essence, the sperm donor is a ghostly figure best kept secret and forgotten, yet haunting the donor-conceived person for life.[71]

The *News-Week* article reported that the successful AID pregnancy resulted in twin girls. The story, which also appeared in newspapers such as *The New York Times* and *The Chicago Tribune*, caused an uproar in the United States.

Not only did the article shine a spotlight on what was a controversial medical procedure at the time, in disclosing the identities of the once-childless couple, Mr. and Mrs. Salvatore Lauricella, as well as the treating physician, Dr. Francis Seymour, it broke one of the cardinal tenets of AID, the physician's code of secrecy. However, it wasn't Dr. Seymour who initially went public with the story, but the Lauricellas. They were so overjoyed by the birth of their daughters that they agreed to be interviewed by the press.

Although Dr. Seymour did give an interview, she defended her actions by blaming the voracious journalists who stormed her office after learning of the AID twins. As a proponent of AID and eugenics, Seymour probably saw this as an opportunity to promote the medical procedure as a safe alternative for infertile couples. At the time, according to *News-Week*, there were only 150 children born annually from AID in the United States.[72]

Putting aside Dr. Seymour's possible breach of medical ethics, the article encapsulates the legal, social, and cultural issues surrounding the burgeoning science of artificial insemination by donor before and after World War II. These issues would continue into the twenty-first century.

For all of Dr. Seymour's forthrightness, she never disclosed the sperm donor's identity. She stated that she chose her sperm donors from a list of blood donors who "will never know the names of the mothers of their flesh and blood children." Donor selection consisted of matching the donor's blood type with the husband's blood type. Her methodology was to collect sperm from three different men, ensuring that only she knew who the father was. Thus, she acted as the sole decider of the genetic fate of the unborn child.[73]

Trusting implicitly in Dr. Seymour's judgment, Mrs. and Mrs. Lauricella would also never know who the biological father of their daughters was. And the twin girls, Victoria and Marylyn, would never know the identity of their ghost father, whose genetics they carried and passed down to their offspring for all future generations. A daunting thought.

This provocative nomenclature, "ghost fathers," will become for donor-conceived people one of the overriding questions of their existence: *Who is my donor father?*

Their parents, who themselves were caught in the web of secrecy instilled in them by their physicians, had no means to help them resurrect these ghostly fathers, even if they wanted to. Not until another technology (commercial DNA tests) became widely available did many donor-conceived people discover that the man who raised them was not their birth father. However, the same technology that revealed the shocking news would also offer them help and hope.

Why the Secrecy?

For moral, psychological, and legal reasons, the donor father was meant to be anonymous, unknown to the childless couple and the resulting child, and in many cases even the treating physician. To blur paternity, some physicians mixed the donor sperm with the husband's sperm, others used two separate donors on alternative days during the woman's ovulatory period.[74]

The importance of donor anonymity was explained in a 1959 article in *The Eugenics Review* by Philip Bloom, MB, ChB, "Artificial Insemination (Donor)," which also defended the use of donor conception as an ethical, moral, and desirable form of medical therapy if it was in harmony with the couple and the doctor.[75] The article outlined the reasons why donor anonymity was crucial for both the parents and the child.

Bloom states: "I prefer that absolutely nobody but the parents themselves and myself should know of the insemination therapy. My last advice to the parents is that under no circumstances should they, or need they, ever tell the child the method of conception—in fact they should forget about it themselves."

How do you forget that you used AID and that there is every possibility the child isn't biologically related to the father? Does the intense overriding desire to have a child supersede every other concern?

This forced amnesia was thought to preserve the marriage and integrate the child into the family. In this way, the integrity of the American family unit would never be challenged.

To help ensure the donor-conceived child's smooth integration into the family unit, many physicians during this time period tried to match the physical characteristics of the donor to the potential parents, taking into account race and ethnicity. (This is similar to the matching paradigm used in placing children with adoptive parents.)

However, physical matching wasn't always possible. Because sperm banks weren't available until the early 1970s, in response to the HIV/AIDs epidemic, physicians had only one option: fresh sperm. Complicating the procedure, ideally, insemination needed to occur when the woman was ovulating. However, locating a sperm donor who was both available to donate and a physical match to the father and/or parents sometimes proved difficult.

Several of the donor-conceived people I interviewed, who didn't physically resemble their parents, said that they were painfully aware that they looked different from their family. Yet, when they asked why they didn't look like other family members, their parents reassured them that they were their child.

Bloom also states that he maintains anonymity between patient and donor. And, like Dr. Seymour, he never tells the donor if the insemination was successful. To maintain this anonymity, he keeps no record of which donor came for which patients. He gave no reason why he preferred it that way.[76]

Peter Boni, himself a donor-conceived person, says in his book *Uprooted*, that to ensure anonymity and secrecy, "less than one-third of those doctors kept records on either the donor or the children resulting from the use of artificial insemination by donor."[77]

Several of the donor-conceived interviewees verified this lack of record-keeping. When they questioned their parents about papers they signed and accessing the medical records, they were told that they didn't have copies of the permission forms, had a vague memory of what was on the form, and in many cases, the fertility clinic, if it still existed, had no records of the procedure.

One donor-conceived interviewee explained, "It was common practice in the 1950s to provide little or no information to the mother and/or couple."

With scant medical records, total anonymity, and no legal recourse, people who discovered they were donor conceived were left in a genetic limbo.

Legality and Morality

Although AID was scientifically revolutionary in the field of infertility treatment, early on and well into the twentieth century, it raised moral and legal questions.

Was being impregnated by another man's sperm an act of adultery by the wife? If so, was the resulting child a bastard? What protection was there against blackmail from sperm donors? Then there was the embarrassment to the sterile man.

The 1934 *News-Week* article cited a legal form that attempted to address the legal status of the child and the relationship of the infertile husband to the child. According to the article, before an infertile couple was referred to a physician for treatment, the husband was required to sign a form.[78]

The document stated that the husband requests of his own free will that the doctor artificially inseminate his wife with the sperm of a male to be selected by the doctor. The form also considered the status of the donor-conceived child.

"Whatever offspring will result from this treatment will be accepted by me as my own."

The husband's agreeing to accept the child as his own prevented the child from being labeled illegitimate.

Regardless of this required document, society as a whole had yet to reckon with the legal and moral conundrums embedded in AID (adultery, illegitimacy, and the husband's obligation to the child).

In terms of morality and religion, the Roman Catholic Church condemned AID as immoral, viewing it as a transgression of the sacredness of the marriage act. All biomedical issues relating to infertility treatment were addressed by the church in 1987 in the *Donum Vitae* document, which is the "Instruction on Respect for Human Life and its Origin and on the Dignity of Procreation." The document stated that: "If . . . the procedure were to replace the conjugal act, it is morally illicit. Artificial Insemination as a substitute for the conjugal act is prohibited." The Catholic Church still views AID as immoral.[79]

One of the donor-conceived interviewee's parents suffered a tragic consequence trying to conceive a child naturally because of a Catholic religious stricture. The husband, who was to receive cancer treatment, was advised by his physician that the treatment could cause sterility and that he should store his sperm. As practicing Catholics, they conferred with their parish priest about the procedure. The priest told them that the means to obtain the sperm (masturbation) went against Catholic teachings. The man's cancer treatment did cause sterility, making it impossible for the couple to conceive a child.

Legally, AID wasn't tested in the courts until 1945 when a Chicago judge set a legal precedent. A 1945 *Time* magazine article titled "Medicine: Artificial Bastards?" delves into whether AID was legally considered adultery. After World War II, veteran Frank Hoch returned home from his tour to find his wife Lorraine two months pregnant. He sued her for divorce. She claimed the baby was artificially conceived.

Judge Feinberg granted the divorce, but on other non-disclosed incriminating evidence. He ruled that AID is legally insufficient for a divorce on grounds of adultery. Feinberg's 1945 ruling established the first precedent for AID,[80] but the conflicting and mystifying legal landscape regarding AID continued all the way through the 1970s.

In *Uprooted*, Peter Boni outlines the discrepancies in the US and abroad: "In 1956 the Illinois Superior Court ruled in *Doornbos v.*

Doornbos that a child conceived via artificial insemination by donor was indeed illegitimate, but that a consenting husband was held liable for that child's support. . . . A 1958 Scottish court ruled that a child from artificial insemination by donor was considered protected under the laws of adoption. A 1963 Superior Court in New York legitimized children of the 'semi-adoption' process of artificial insemination by donor."[81]

Not until the 1980s did certain states mandate the legal status of AID children to be legitimate. Furthermore, out of an abundance of caution, six states stipulated that the procedure had to be performed by a physician.[82] Currently, the legal status of AID children is a state-by-state issue, as is the right for donor-conceived people to find his or her donor.

However, the United Kingdom recently passed legislation that will allow donor-conceived young adults born after a certain date to discover their biological origins.

According to the *Guardian*, "[t]he changes will make it possible for most people conceived from egg, sperm, or embryo donations made after 1 April 2005 to request identifiable information after they turn 14. This includes their donor's full name, date of birth, and last known address."[83]

There is no such federal law in the United States. Kara Rubinstein Deyerin, CEO and founder of Right To Know, is working to have legislature passed in all fifty states that would allow donor-conceived people access to their genetic identities.

But for now, many donor-conceived people seeking their biological fathers have no recourse other than hiring a genealogy geneticist, contacting DNAngels (a search organization that helps people find biological parents using DNA and research), or conduct their own detective work using sites such as Ancestry and 23andMe to find their ghost fathers.

Fertility Fraud: Crossing the Line

As more people are finding through DNA tests that they were artificially conceived, some are also finding that they share the same sperm donor with multiple people.

Even more shocking and horrifying, others are discovering that their sperm donor was their mother's fertility doctor. In the last few years, these stories of treating physicians who crossed an ethical and legal line to impregnate their patients without their consent are coming to light, demonstrating the need for regulation.

The documentary film, *Our Father* (2022), chronicles a much-publicized case of fertility fraud committed by the infamous fertility specialist Dr. Donald Cline (Indiana). From 1979 to 1986, he inseminated dozens of patients with his own sperm and without their knowledge or consent. His patients were told he was using frozen sperm from a registered sperm bank or that it was their husband's sperm.[84] At the time of the documentary's release, ninety-four biological children of Dr. Cline had been identified. There are sure to be more.

His appalling actions were first discovered in 2014 by Jacoba Ballard when she took a commercial DNA test and found she had seven half-siblings, all the biological offspring of Cline. As additional half-siblings were uncovered, she took on the onerous task of informing the new siblings.

"I know every time I call a new sibling, I'm going to ruin their life," she said, expressing the trauma unleashed by Cline. It was Ballard who eventually went to a news outlet to expose Cline's criminal act.

Another half-sibling, Julie Harmon, said of her loss of self, "it completely washes away your identity. You really have no idea who you are anymore."

What's especially sickening, as depicted in the documentary, is that he masturbated in a nearby bathroom before inserting his newly harvested semen into his patients via artificial insemination. It's difficult not to view this as rape.

Cline's defense was he thought he was helping women who wanted a baby. The film suggests his reasons were tied to his religious beliefs.

In 2017, a criminal investigation against Cline was launched. When charges were finally brought against him, it wasn't for rape. It was for two counts of felony obstruction of justice, for lying during the investigation. He pled guilty and received no jail time, only a $500 fine.[85]

A *Newsweek* article highlighted the evidence that was brought against him: "[he] could not be criminally charged, even when two paternity tests filed as evidence in his criminal case named Cline as the biological father of two of his patient's children."[86]

Just as there is no federal law regulating sperm donations, there is no law criminalizing the act of a doctor inseminating a patient with his own sperm without their consent.

Incensed by the injustice, the siblings and parents lobbied for a fertility fraud law, criminalizing fertility fraud. In 2018, Indiana became the first state in the United States to make it illegal for fertility doctors to use their own sperm without the patient's consent.

However, there is no federal law that makes insemination by the treating doctor a criminal offense. As of 2023, only eleven states have fertility fraud laws: Arkansas, Arizona, California, Colorado, Florida, Indiana, Kentucky, Illinois, Ohio, Texas, and Utah. Depending on the particular state, only some consider fertility fraud a felony.[87]

As author Peter Boni points out, "There is more legislation protecting unborn dogs and puppy breeding that there is for the entire reproductive industry."[88]

Although Cline may be the most well-known case of fertility fraud, he's not alone. *The New York Times* reported in 2022 that in the last several years, at least fifty doctors in the United States have been accused of fraud in connection with donating their sperm to their patients, not including those accused in 2023 in Vermont and Washington. Not surprisingly, the majority of physicians who have been accused of fertility fraud were discovered as a result of a DNA test.[89]

A 2022 *New York Times* article on fertility fraud cited several fertility specialists who used their own sperm to impregnate their patients. Dr. Robert Tichell, a retired fertility specialist, stated that he did it out of necessity. He claimed that the women were anxious to get pregnant, and timing was crucial. If he couldn't get a donor, he resorted to using his own sperm. He assumed other doctors did the same thing, though no one talked about it.

Tichell said, "It wasn't exactly ethical, but it wasn't unknown to happen." In a later text to a *New York Times* reporter who covered the story, he elaborated.

"It may have been less than perfect, but with luck, the women were able to conceive."[90]

Wasn't exactly ethical? Less than perfect? This was another case of the ends justifying the means with little to no thought of the consequences to the mothers and their children. His tone-deaf response illustrates his and other perpetrating doctors' lack of understanding of the trauma they inflicted.

In the same *New York Times* article, Traci Portugal, who runs the website DonorDeceived.org, gave an insightful explanation of how these doctors justified committing fertility fraud:

> *For some doctors, I think there was a disconnect between this being a medical procedure and the fact that they were creating and giving away their own children. For others, they knew what they were doing was wrong, and they were able to hide their predatory sexual actions behind the use of anonymity.*

Fertility fraud is not confined to the United States. A notorious case in Canada of fertility doctor Norman Barwin, involving 226 former patients and their children, led to a class action suit. It was Canada's first legal settlement of its kind. The families accepted about $13 million in compensation. The largest settlement in Canada's history.[91]

We Are Making Humans

When artificial insemination by donor first became a viable medical treatment for infertility, no one could have foreseen that commercial DNA tests would lift the veil of secrecy surrounding the procedure, leaving donor-conceived people bewildered, betrayed, and searching for their ghost fathers. And no one could have foreseen the abuses that would occur because of this secrecy.

On the Right to Know website section, "The Fighting Fertility Fraud Act of 2023," it estimates that 1 in 27 people in the United States are conceived through assisted reproduction. The site points out that fraud can occur in any aspect of the assisted reproduction process, and it occurs more than we think.[92]

> *Just once is one time too many—we are making humans. Gamete providers lie about their medical, identity, and background information to entice recipient parents to use their specimen. Having incorrect information can lead to premature death and unnecessary illness of offspring. Clinics do not always use the gametes patients request and they make false statements to gamete providers and recipient parents.*

The trauma of discovering as adults that you are a victim of fertility fraud wreaks devastation on donor-conceived people's psyche, scarring them for life. Their very existence becomes tinged with deceit and betrayal.

* All the interviewees in this section have opted to use a pseudonym.

CHAPTER 18

Forty-Nine and Counting
The Strange Story of the Many, Many Half-Siblings

"I know this woman from work who was conceived by artificial insemination," my friend texts me in early March 2022.

A strange opening to a text, but she knows I'm looking for parental discovery stories. I'm at the beginning of the project. So far, I've interviewed three people. None were donor conceived.

"And get this," the text continues. "Her sperm donor donated multiple times. Not sure how many, but let's just say she has a lot of siblings. Are you interested?"

My fingers can't type fast enough.

"Yes. Thanks. Please do an email intro. What's her name?"

"Robin."

"How you'd find this out?"

I wait, watching the text dots pulse. When her message appears, I'm intrigued.

"When I mentioned your project to her, she just blurted it out. I had no idea. And she told me that this happened in Chicago over many years."

As far as I know, no stories of multiple sperm donations in the Chicago area have been reported.

Once Robin gives permission for me to contact her, I email her immediately. I explain the project and tell her about my book *White Like Her*, and my own discovery story. The following day, she emails me back:

> *It would be an honor to talk with you about the somewhat strange situation surrounding my many, MANY, discovered half-siblings. Attached is a timeline of those who we know of so far, who, thanks to artificial insemination practices at the time, have the same biological father.*

Surprisingly, she tells me the biological father's name. But then she adds a caveat. "Please keep this document, and the names of those listed in the document and in my mailbox below—CONFIDENTIAL."

I look at the birth year timeline—last revised September 6, 2022. Across the page are a succession of multi-colored arrows in rows pointing to the right. Inside each arrow is a half-sibling's name and birth year, with several exceptions. The document indicates that there are five sets of full siblings, which means that their mothers were inseminated by the same sperm donor.

The birth dates range from 1954 to 1981. I'm astounded by the time span.

In a later timeline, (revised June 30, 2023), Robin includes a head shot of the donor father. When I interview his offspring, I refer to that photo, comparing their physical features with his, as well as comparing their resemblances to each other. In some cases, their resemblances to each other are so marked it's obvious that they're siblings.

Robin's first email will be the first of many attesting to her commitment to helping me accurately tell this unique and amazing story. One of the reasons she wants this story made public is that she wants people to know nothing illegal was done. There was no fertility fraud.

"Nothing unethical was done here. The donor father was not the treating doctor." Then she adds. "Sperm had to be 'fresh' back then."

Wanting me to understand the dilemma faced by her half-siblings, especially those born in the 1950s, she explains that not only did they have no idea they were the product of a sperm donor, but by the time they found out, their parents and siblings had died and they had no one to ask about this well-kept secret.

"This has been a very difficult path for some of them. Some were devasted, angry, shocked, and in complete denial," she explains.

Then she casually mentions that, thanks to one of the half-siblings who fettered out the name of their sperm donor and made contact with one of the sperm donor's sons, the group has an "unbelievably great relationship" with the sperm donor's first wife and two of his three natural children.

"We get together for a pool party annually at the daughter's house. It still freaks me out. You can't make this stuff up."

My mind goes spinning off as I try to imagine this group of strangers meeting for the first time at the house of the sperm donor's natural daughter. It seems unreal, and contradicts everything in the newspaper accounts I've read about siblings conceived from the same sperm donor.

How have they been able to form this strong bond out of what, for some donor-conceived people with the same donor, is not only traumatic, but alienating?

Robin ends her email by telling me she'll have to get permission from the others before putting me in contact with them, which I expected.

"We're a closed group who communicate through Facebook Messenger and are very respectful of each other's privacy," she states. Then she suggests we speak before I contact any of them to discuss who in the group would be the most appropriate to interview.

During our phone conversation I explain how, after *White Like Her* was published and I appeared on *The Today Show*, I received and continue to receive emails from strangers needing to share their secrets, which became the impetus for this project.

I tell her that the project is meant to help people who discover as adults that they're not who they thought they were; that, because of commercial DNA tests, more and more people are making these discoveries; and that I believe we all have the right to know where we came from.

After we speak, she sends out a group email that explains what my book is about, asking if anyone would like to share their story with me.

The following week Robin emails me excerpts of the "detective" work done by one of the half-siblings, who tracked down the identity of the sperm donor. Again, she cautions me to keep this information confidential.

Over the next few months, Robin puts me in contact with the half-siblings willing to share their stories, vouching for my credibility and intentions. These half-siblings' (Sara, Tom, and Ellen) fascinating narratives appear in Chapters 20, 21, and 22.

Robin also reveals the extraordinary circumstances that led to their annual pool parties at the sperm donor's daughter's house, and how the half-siblings bonded together.

Taking a philosophical, almost transcendent viewpoint, Robin says: "We all agree that there is a reason we have found each other at this time of our lives."

The School of Genetic Revelations

When Robin first learned she had biological half-siblings, there were seven known offspring of the sperm donor listed on Ancestry.com. Within nine months, from September 2017 to May 2018, the headcount went from seven to eighteen (not including the sperm donor's three children).

One of the first identified half-siblings from the original seven volunteered to take on the difficult task of identifying the sperm donor. In a detailed account that reads like detective fiction, he outlined how he found the sperm donor, now deceased. (This individual hasn't given permission to share how he tracked down the sperm donor.) Once he identified the sperm donor, he contacted one of the sperm donor's sons, who, in turn, contacted his mother. She confirmed that her ex-husband had been a sperm donor.

Upon confirmation, the half-sibling who did the detective work asked the natural son if he would send him a photo of his biological father, and if he could share it with the group. The son agreed. Once the sperm donor's identity and photo were given to the other half-siblings, they started to get to know each other, exchanging photos and information about themselves. It seems knowing who their biological father was and seeing his image began their process of bonding.

"We learned that some of our mothers had seen the same OB/ GYN and gave birth to us at the same hospital," Robin writes.

"One of the half-siblings, who was born in the 1970s and whose mother is still living, told her that her father had to sign an agreement that he would never 'disown or disinherit' the child conceived through AID. Her parents were told never to tell anyone about the procedure to protect the donor and their families."

In their excitement about finding each other and learning the identity of their sperm donor, they decided to have a get-together over Memorial Day weekend in the Chicago area.

Robin, who plans business dinners and caters meetings as part of her job, offered to handle the event's logistics, from booking a restaurant to putting together a half-sibling collage.

"I think the event planners were more excited than I was when I explained the reason for our gathering," Robin says, "I sent out a questionnaire to everyone asking about their story and how/when they came to learn their father was not their father. I also asked them to send photos of themselves as children and adults, and their families."

However, the most unexpected and surreal surprise happened a few days before the event. In an extraordinary act of kindness and generosity, the sperm donor's former wife emailed the half-sibling who'd done the detective work saying that she would attend the event and bring family photographs.

Robin describes the ex-wife as beyond wonderful. She told the group that no question was off limits. She brought photo albums, gave them background information about the sperm donor, including his medical history. She reiterated that she was aware of what he was doing, and that he believed he was doing a good deed.

If her husband gave them the gift of life, she gave them the gift of knowing who he was.

At the get-together, some of the half-siblings referred to each other as brother and sister. But Robin said she wasn't comfortable with that. She told them that her sisters were the siblings she grew up and shared a family history with. To her, the half-siblings were friends, sort of like classmates.

"After all, we all recently graduated from the School of Genetic Revelation," she jokes.

Afterward, Robin thought that would be the end of it.

"We really just wanted to see if we looked alike, had the same mannerisms. I truly thought this was going to be a 'one and done' deal."

However, in spite of Robin's doubts, that's not what happened.

Instead of a "one and done," they organized. The half-siblings designated one person as their "ambassador." That person was in charge of contacting half-siblings who showed up as "Close Family" on Ancestry and/or 23andMe. They created a message to post when a newbie appeared on the genealogical sites.

The message was supportive and mysterious:

> *You probably noticed that there are several Close Family members listed in your profile. Many of us have connected and we have additional information regarding this situation. If you're interested, we would be happy to provide additional information.*

I imagine it must be mind-blowing to receive that message. I would wonder, *what is 'this situation'? Who are these people to me? If my parents are deceased, who would I turn to?*

Because the group emails were becoming cumbersome, a Facebook Messenger group was set up for basic communication. Included in this closed group were the sperm donor's ex-wife and children.

Robin handled the timeline, keeping it updated by adding new half-siblings with their permission as they appeared. The group's "ambassador" created a map showing where everyone was located in the US. (Currently, half-siblings live in thirteen different states.)

Zoom calls were scheduled several times a year depending on how many newbies showed up and were interested in meeting their half-siblings.

However, the most astonishing result of that first meeting was what the natural daughter of the sperm donor did. After contact was made with the donor's family, the following summer, she invited everyone to her house for a weekend get-together—a ritual that has continued until the present day. Those who can't attend participate via Zoom.

One of the half-siblings I interviewed referred to her first trip to meet the other half-siblings at the daughter's house, as "a pilgrimage."

Although the forty-nine-and-counting group of half-siblings have bonded, the fact remains that their shared donor-conceived paternity poses difficult psychological and relational questions, not easily answered or navigated. How do we look at AID half-siblings? Are they family? Are they friends? Where do they fit into each other's lives?

In some cases, they don't fit into their lives. Not all the half-siblings who are contacted by the group's "ambassador" opt to be an active part of the group. Blood isn't enough to bind them.

As for those who have embraced their half-siblings, how do they view their sperm donor father? Are the same rituals, such as visiting a parent's grave, afforded to him?

In 2019, some of that first group of half-siblings visited the sperm donor's grave. One had written him a letter. All of them placed a stone on his headstone out of respect and gratitude to a man they will never know who gave them life.

Robin wrote in one of her reflective emails:

> *The initial revelation brings about a whole range of emotions. Many were happy to learn that they have what they call a 'bonus family.' A handful are still in denial despite the science. I cannot imagine how I would feel if I had known nothing. Every doctor and hospital visit includes more and more questions about our medical history. Even if you know about the AI, half of it is missing. If you didn't know, half of what you tell the doctor is incorrect and irrelevant.*

However, their ghost father is integrated into their altered reality, his genetic sway is profound and everlasting. Every day of their lives, they carry his legacy, and those who have children pass that legacy on to their children.

* The people in the next four chapters (Robin, Sara, Tom, and Ellen) are half-siblings and part of the forty-nine-and-counting group. Bridget, from Chapter 23, had a different sperm donor and a very different experience than the half-siblings group.

CHAPTER 19

Three Sisters, Three Secrets
Robin (born 1959)

ROBIN, MY LIAISON WITH THE HALF-SIBLINGS, BEGINS OUR INTERVIEW WITH a harrowing story.

We had to delay our meeting because her husband had been hospitalized for two weeks and had just returned home. She tells me in a halting, yet steady voice that, while he was in the hospital, his sister was rushed to the same hospital. As he slept in the intensive care unit recovering, she coded and died. The shock of her death sent the family reeling.

"We told my husband the next day. It was hard to see her go," Robin says.

Behind her is a curio cabinet, photos line two walls. None are clearly visible.

Her sister-in-law's death has nothing to do with her being one of forty-nine half-siblings from the same donor—the story I've come to hear. It has to do with the alchemy that occurs when you enter another's story, another's life. What happens when art and life collide.

She and I have forged a bond over the past four months, as she reached out to her half-siblings on my behalf, as the business of the book shifted to the business of living, of being human. The boundaries blur and I enter with my own story, sharing with her my husband's life-threatening kidney cancer surgery over twenty-three years ago, letting her know I've been there, that I understand what she's going through.

After Robin tells me about the eerie circumstances of her husband and sister-in-law in the same hospital, as one recovers and the other doesn't, she says "I gotta tell you, you can't make this stuff up, Gail."

You can't make this stuff up will be the mantra for Robin's story and every story in this book, including my own. Faced with unfathomable and unexpected discoveries, we can only concede to the unreality that is our reality.

I'm taken back to that cold January in 1995 when I sat outside the Family History Center, after having discovered my mother's Black family, staring at my reflection in the car's rearview mirror, wondering what just happened. *And who the hell am I now?*

That Shut Me Up

Robin's discovery began with an argument.

"I was maybe fifteen. My mother and I were arguing. I was giving her a hard time. You know, typical teenage stuff.

"She got so angry with me, she said, 'I don't know why I bothered to go through all that trouble to be artificially inseminated to have you.'

"That shut me up," she says. "That's really all I remember. In that moment, I was shocked. I think I repressed a lot of what happened after that."

Why that day? Why in that moment did Robin's mother choose to blurt out a secret she'd kept for over fifteen years? Does the secret become too heavy to carry? Robin can only speculate. She never asked her before she passed, and now it's too late.

In one horrifying moment, Robin learned not only that the man who raised her wasn't her father, but that her biological father was an anonymous sperm donor—a man she most likely would never know. No wonder she repressed much of what happened afterwards.

One thing she didn't repress and remembers vividly is not feeling sad about the revelation.

"I can't say I was sad. My parents had been divorced for three years when this happened. My father was not a nice man. It wasn't like he beat me or anything like that. He was just mean and crabby. He made us all miserable."

She relates a painful interaction between her and her father when her parents were separated.

"I was twelve. He sat me down at my grandmother's kitchen table, threw the divorce papers in front of me, and yelled, 'You could stop this! If you tell your mother that you don't want the divorce, she will listen to you.' I wasn't going to do that. All I knew was he made my mother cry."

She takes a deep breath.

"So, there you have it. Blame the kid because you couldn't keep your marriage together."

"Did you ever have any inkling your father wasn't your father?"

I want to see if her mother had dropped any clues about Robin's paternity.

"People made comments that my two sisters and I didn't look alike. And we don't. Some people outright asked my mother if we were adopted. No one said anything about artificial insemination."

Not surprising, given how uncommon AID was in 1959 when Robin was born.

When she asked her mother if she was adopted, her mother answered emphatically: "Trust me, you were not adopted."

Was her mother hinting at the truth of Robin's conception?

Throughout my childhood, my mother dropped subtle clues about her own racial heritage, telling me about the horrible way Black people were treated in New Orleans during the Jim Crow era. Looking back on her stories, I believe she was hinting at her true identity, savoring her racial secret, yet not wanting to reveal it for fear of the consequences.

A few days after Robin learned the truth of her conception, her mother talked to her three daughters separately. She had two more secrets to reveal. Robin's middle sister was also conceived via artificial insemination by donor, but the youngest wasn't. The covert nature of the conception and the accompanying cover-up stun me.

"My youngest sister was the product of an affair. Talk about keeping secrets. My mother told me that she asked the doctor not to tell her husband about her affair. So, to explain the unexpected pregnancy, the doctor told her husband that it was a one-in-a-million chance, assuring him that the child was indeed his."

Did the doctor's decision fall under the purview of patient confidentiality? What about the unsuspecting father? Did the doctor have an obligation to tell him the child wasn't his? Was the doctor, in essence, a co-conspirator in the deception?

I ask Robin how her mother was able to convince her fertility doctor to lie to her husband. Before answering, she clarifies that the doctor wasn't her fertility doctor, but her obstetrician. He arranged for her to take part in a fertility study at a Chicago hospital, which resulted in her first two children.

"There were a lot of 'family closet' secrets back then. And there wasn't any DNA to prove otherwise," Robin says.

Then she adds, "He probably wanted to keep her as a patient."

Growing up, Robin always felt her youngest sister was favored by her father because she was the baby and was really cute, but it was really because he thought she was the only child who was his biologically.

According to Robin's middle sister, after the truth came out, their mother made the youngest sister swear to never tell their father about her being another man's child. Robin says she doesn't recall her and her two sisters ever discussing the situation among themselves until after they had all moved out of their mother's house.

Robin is convinced her father went to his grave never knowing the truth of his youngest child's paternity. She's also convinced he believed that Robin and her middle sister didn't know that they were donor conceived.

Not long after the revelation, Robin's mother told her a strange incident that occurred while she was pregnant with Robin.

"While sleeping, my mother woke twice to find my father wielding his arm to hit her in the stomach. She said he did this in his sleep and must have been unconsciously resentful of her carrying another man's child." Then Robin adds, "Over the years, my mother told me many strange stories."

Whether the story was true or not, it reveals as much about her mother as her father. Was her mother conflicted about carrying another man's child? Had her father made some sly comment about the pregnancy? He knew that his wife had received fertility treatment. If he was resentful, was his resentment because, at the time, he believed that he was infertile?

Over the years, as Robin got older, her mother would share some of the intimate details of her father's infertility and the artificial insemination procedure she received.

Infertility and Secrets

Infertility and secrets abound in Robin's family. Her father's two sisters weren't able to have children. So, all her cousins on her father's side are adopted. Her father was the family's only hope for a son to carry on the family name. Because of his low sperm count, he tried an experimental drug to help increase his sperm count, but the drug had the opposite effect. Although the family was aware of his sisters' infertility, his infertility was kept secret.

Rather than adopt, Robin's parents chose artificial insemination because they wanted everyone to think that their children were all "blood related."

Maintaining the illusion of blood children reflects the societal ideals of the time. During the 1950s and the early 1960s the nuclear family, consisting of a married couple, and their blood children, was held up as the ideal family structure. Men were the breadwinners and women looked after the children and did housework. In this idyllic societal view of family, not being able to have children was viewed as a failing.[93]

Robin says that her mother once said that she wondered what great sin her husband's family had committed that none of their three children were able to conceive.

"Big shame back then, if you didn't have kids right away," Robin explains. "I wasn't born until five years after they were married. So, I'm sure there was some suspicion."

Robin's mother painted a vivid picture of her AID procedure, which took place in the late 1950s. As mentioned previously, at that time, there were no sperm banks. Only fresh sperm was available. Her mother was instructed to take her temperature daily. When her temperature was elevated, she was instructed to phone her doctor immediately. She remarked that every time she called her doctor, he was frantic and would say, "Where am I going to find a donor at such short notice?"

But he told her to come in anyway and that he would find one. Depending on which facility the doctor was practicing at that day, she'd either take a bus or an expensive, hour-long taxi ride.

Her mother was convinced that her treating doctor was the sperm donor. Even though Robin and her middle sister look nothing alike, Robin assumed her mother was right. And if her mother wasn't right, there was no way for Robin to find out who her biological father was, at least not until commercial DNA tests became mainstream. However, her reasons for taking the DNA test were two-fold and had nothing to do with finding her biological father:

"After seeing tons of commercials on Ancestry, in May 2017, I purchased two kits—one for myself and one for my middle sister. I wanted to see if we shared the same sperm donor father. But more importantly, I wanted my complete medical history, which was becoming more and more significant to me. My mom had all these medical issues. But what about my father's side? I was concerned not only for myself, but for my sons and grandson."

What she discovered changed the trajectory of her life.

Close Family?

The results of Robin and her AID-conceived sister's DNA tests proved disappointing. They didn't share the same sperm donor. In fact, her sister had only one "Close Family" match. And it was Robin. They shared 1529 centimorgans (cMs) on the maternal side and no cMs on the paternal side, making them half-siblings. Full siblings share a range of 2,400 to 2,800 cMs. (A close family match on Ancestry can be an aunt, uncle, niece (1301–2193 centimorgans), nephew, grandparent, grandchild, half-sibling (1320–2134), double-first cousin, first cousin (very unlikely, but possible).[94]

Robin, on the other hand, had seven people listed on her profile as "Close Family, including her sister." She didn't know who the other six people were and didn't think much about it. She was only seeking information about her sister and her medical history.

"I thought the other 'Close Family' matches were cousins. It never crossed my mind they were half-siblings," she says. She soon found out who these six mysterious people were.

On September 12, 2017, one of the people listed on Robin's Ancestry profile contacted her. He'd found her on Facebook and asked if she would call him. She did.

His first question to her was: Did she know what "Close Family" meant when the match was about 1300 centimorgans or more?

She said no.

"It means I'm your half-brother. And all of the others listed on both of our profiles are half-siblings."

He promised to email her the information another half-sibling had gathered that would help explain everything. She also learned that there were more half-siblings on other websites, such as Family Tree DNA.

Robin says, "I remember my brain going a million miles an hour and being very tense. I remember not sleeping. You don't really know what to think, what this does to your life, and what are you supposed to do about it?"

Over the next few months, more names appeared on Ancestry as "Close Family." However, the identity of their sperm donor remained elusive. One of the half-siblings speculated that it might be the treating doctor. Another half-sibling questioned that assumption, based on the treating doctor's spotless reputation, and took on the role of "detective" and accepted the arduous task of trying to identify their sperm donor.

Prior to our interview, Robin emailed me the very thorough investigative work the half-sibling had done. As a mystery author and avid reader of mysteries, I was impressed by his dogged research and methodology, which read like a mystery novel. Only instead of hunting down a murderer, he was hunting down the man who gave him and his half-siblings life. (As stated in the prior chapter, I don't have permission to share his research.)

On January 30, 2018, the "detective" sent a group email, announcing he had identified the sperm donor, who unfortunately was deceased. Finally, the half-siblings knew who their "ghost" father was. It wasn't Robin's mother's treating doctor, as she'd assumed. However, it was too late for Robin to tell her the donor's identity. Her mother died in the spring of 2017.

The news ignited the half siblings. A flurry of email ensued, brimming with family photos, birth certificates, and other personal information. They were eager to know each other.

In February, Robin asked the group of half-siblings if they would be interested in getting together in person.

"I knew we really wanted to see if we looked alike and had the same mannerisms. We were curious as to how our shared genes came into play. After all, half of our genes, half of who we are genetically, came from the same man."

Once the Memorial Day get together was finalized, Robin told her children about their grandfather. Her oldest son thanked her. He'd just submitted his, his wife's, and their son's DNA samples to 23andMe because they'd discovered one of their children had sickle cell anemia.

The results showed that Robin's son was 30 percent Ashkenazi Jewish. "If you hadn't told me, I would have asked you who you were sleeping with. We know dad isn't Jewish," her son joked.

A few days before the party, two unexpected things happened. A new sibling popped up, which brought the total number of known half-siblings to eighteen. Within nine months, from September 2017 when Robin first learned of her half-siblings to May 2018, the get-together date, the half-siblings group went from seven to eighteen.

Is DNA family?

It goes without saying that discovering you have forty-nine (and potentially more) half-siblings is a life-altering occurrence, affecting not just the individual, but their family as well.

Robin says it's taken her time to process what's happened and to find a way to integrate this "new family" into her life. Comparing Robin's story with the two newer half-siblings, Tom and Ellen, it's clear that being a part of this unusually supportive group has been instrumental in helping Robin adjust to her new reality, and most likely will do the same for the two newer half-siblings.

After the get-together, Robin mentioned to a co-worker how much she liked these people; how they're so much easier to be with than her own family. Her co-worker responded, "But you didn't go through the hard stuff with them, like sickness and burying parents."

"I hadn't thought of it that way. But my friend was right. We've never done anything that was hard. It's only DNA that links us as family. There is no history here, no burden of the past with its hurts and crises, with its jealousies and longing for love. It's DNA without history. What we share are chromosomes, multi-colored beads on a chain. Yes, we're starting a new history as a group. But it's not the same as being born into a family and growing up with someone."

As the interview winds down, I ask Robin if she's better off knowing or not knowing.

"Well, now I know my medical history, which was important to me," she replies.

"I know I'm part Jewish, which has given me a sense of peace. I think I always knew deep down that I wasn't solely a Catholic."

She pauses for a moment.

"But I also think the truth doesn't always set you free," she adds. "Sometimes it just causes even more confusion. Even with the confusion, I'm grateful that we found each other. And I believe there's a reason we found each other at this time in our lives."

CHAPTER 20

———

Never to Know

Sara (born 1958)

SARA IS THE FIRST HALF-SIBLING WHO ANSWERS ROBIN'S GROUP EMAIL. Even before there's a general consensus that real names won't be used, she requests that I not use her real name. Although she seems eager to tell her story.

For the interview, she uses her iPhone, which narrows what I can see of her living room and of her.

Her passion for helping people is evident in her education and profession. It seems engrained in her psyche and possibly in her genetic heritage. All but one of the half-siblings I interviewed are in a helping profession. Sara also holds a BS in psychology, a master's degree in social work, and a certificate in gerontology.

"I always had an interest in psychology in college," she says. "And I was also interested in gerontology. I really like old people. We had a surrogate grandmother/babysitter when we were kids, and she was more of a grandmother than our regular grandmother."

Since the 1980s, Sara has worked at a state mental hospital in various roles within her clinical social work background—from patient work to her current position doing utilization review.

With wry humor, she says, "I'm kind of a fossil."

In 2010, she was diagnosed with rheumatoid arthritis, an autoimmune disease.

"I'll have this for the rest of my life," she explains. "And it's pretty severe."

Since the pandemic, she's been teleworking and although she has a crippling disease, she continues to work full time. "The way I look at it is I'm a valuable person."

Aunt Sara, I Have Some Surprising News

As we move further into the conversation, Sara recalls a watercolor painting that hung in her brother's bedroom. It was of a little boy, laying on his side, holding a balloon. On the balloon were the words NUMBER ONE SON.

"That's how my brother was treated," Sara says. "My mother always favored him. There was a double standard."

She thought maybe it was because he was the only boy.

It wouldn't be until 2019, after her mother's death, when her niece phoned her with unexpected news that led Sara to believe there might be another reason why her brother was favored.

"Aunt Sara, I have some surprising news," she said. "I took one of those DNA tests. Guess what? I'm not related to your brother, my uncle. And even more surprising, there's this half-sibling group that I think you might be related to. Do you want to get tested?"

Sara was in shock. The news seemed incomprehensible. As in so many of these adult discoveries, there was no one in her immediate family to ask. Her parents were dead. Her sister was dead. She was estranged from her brother. So, she took the test.

The results were bittersweet and left her with questions that would never be answered.

"I've come to understand, I'll never know for sure some things," Sara says. "And that troubles me."

Like so many of these DNA surprises, Sara's niece took a DNA test looking for information about her ancestry, never considering that she would uncover an old family secret meant to stay buried.

When Sara's niece received her results, she couldn't understand why she wasn't related to any of her grandfather's family on her maternal side, yet she was related to a lot of people she didn't know. Understandably, she was perplexed and shaken.

Baffled by the results, Sara's niece contacted one of the people listed as a close match. What he told her was even more perplexing: The contact's biological father had been a sperm donor. The number of centimorgans between the contact and Sara's niece indicated that the sperm donor was most likely her maternal grandfather, which would make him her mother's father. Since her own mother was dead and her DNA couldn't be tested, Sara's niece contacted Sara and her maternal uncle. She wanted to know if they were related to the sperm donor.

Sara explains that she took the test for several reasons. She wanted to know with certainty if her father was her biological father. The overriding question for her was: What was the nature of the relationship between her sister and her? Were they full or half-siblings? The answer would determine if she was related to this group of half-siblings, and who her father was.

Whatever the test results showed, the family dynamic was already forever altered—Sara's late sister was the offspring of a sperm donor, not the man who raised them.

Sara's brother's results came first. He was not related to the multiple half-siblings. He was the natural son of his mother and father, not the son of a sperm donor. Perhaps being the favored child had less to do with his gender and more to do with who his father was, Sara reasoned.

Now it was a matter of waiting for Sara's results, which would determine whether her sister was a full sibling or a half-sibling. For several weeks, Sara endeavored to process the possibility that her father might not be her biological father. If it turned out that he wasn't, and the sperm donor was her biological father, she would take comfort in knowing that she and her sister still had the same father.

When the results came, Sara felt numb. She and her sister did have the same biological father. The man she thought was her father suddenly wasn't, and she had a slew of half-siblings.

"But it was sad that my only true 100 percent sibling was deceased," she says.

Once Sara knew that she was related to these strangers, she told her niece that it was okay for the group's "ambassador" and the other half-siblings to contact her.

Her first interaction with one of her new half-siblings was an afternoon phone call that lasted two and a half hours. The woman told her about their biological father—that he had three other natural children, what his profession and medical history were, and the circumstances of his sperm donations (where they took place and over what period of time).

Even with this plethora of information, Sara's half-sibling wasn't able to answer one question that gnawed at her.

"What I wanted to know was what my parents knew about the insemination or didn't know? In other words, what did the fertility clinic tell them?"

She wanted to know whose fault it was for their paternity being kept secret. Was it with the fertility clinic? Or was it with her parents?

The half-sibling "ambassador" couldn't answer that.

That same evening, despite her call running late, Sara attended her monthly book club meeting. Ironically, the book they were discussing that night was *The Girls Who Went Away: The Hidden History of Women Who Surrendered Children for Adoption in the Decades before Roe v. Wade*—a book about family secrets and shame, about young unwed pregnant women who were sent away by their families and forced to give up their babies.[95]

"So, I had this information churning in my head about my own situation and I'm listening to this stuff about these girls who were sent away, then reconnected with the children they gave up," she explains.

It was an emotionally grueling night for Sara. Still processing what she'd learned, she told no one at the book club about her own family secret. Not until the drive home did she reveal everything to her friend: that her biological father was a sperm donor, that she knew his identity, and that she had multiple siblings.

In the ensuing days, her friends rallied around her. One friend, a mycologist who works for the USDA in plant pathology, interpreted her DNA results. Another friend, a retired law professor, sent her a dissertation on artificial insemination practices in the twentieth century that outlined the variety of disclosure and non-disclosure practices that happened in the 1950s, which was of particular interest to Sara. A third friend, who was adopted, was very supportive and continues to be—as are Sara's two nieces, her sister's daughters.

But that lingering question remained: What did her parents know about the insemination treatment?

Since Sara had been told by one of the half-siblings that the majority of the fertility clinic's records were destroyed in a fire, she had no way to find out what forms her parents signed, which would have indicated if they understood the treatment they were receiving. It's possible her parents weren't told they were having an AID procedure. They might have thought they were just getting treatment for infertility.

"My mom may not have even known she was inseminated," Sara says, and this disturbs her. Did her mom know that her father wasn't her biological father? Did she even know she was receiving the AID procedure? And if she knew, did her father know?

The closest she's come to understanding her mother's fertility treatment came from the mother of one of her half-siblings. On her death bed, she confessed that she had had fertility treatment, and that her husband was there and gave a sperm sample. Then, the doctor left the room. When he returned, he had a test tube and was stirring something. He never said anything. Then she received the treatment.

Sara's brother, now her half-brother—who she's been estranged from since their mother's death in 2016—took a more aggressive approach to finding out what their mother knew. According to Sara's nieces, he went to his mother's psychotherapist and asked if his mother had discussed using a sperm donor. Due to patient/client confidentiality, the psychotherapist refused to disclose any information from her private therapy sessions.

Even though Sara has come to terms with never knowing, certain aspects of the secret still linger. She remains perplexed, even troubled, by her mother's silence at a crucial time in her sister's life, a time when knowing who her real father was might have been helpful. Maybe not.

Another Unanswered Question

"This is something you'll probably be interested in. It has to do with my deceased sister," Sara says.

"I don't know if Robin told you about this, but I had a sister who was diagnosed with a bipolar disorder as an adult. She was eighteen months younger than me. We had the same sperm donor."

The implication of genetic inheritance hangs in the air. In suggesting possible half-siblings to interview, Robin had told me about Sara's sister's mental illness and that the sperm donor's mother, their genetic grandmother, had been diagnosed with a bipolar disorder. One of the topics of discussion among the half-siblings was the genetic diseases they might have inherited from their sperm donor.

I'd planned to ask about her sister, but toward the end of the interview when trust had been established between us.

What prompted Sara to broach such a private and painful matter? I wonder.

Was it talking about her work at the state mental hospital and her chronic and severe rheumatoid arthritis, another possible genetic inheritance? Or was it that her sister is never far from her thoughts? Or is it that question—what did her mother know—that never totally leaves her? Embedded in that question is culpability and possible betrayal, all in the name of preserving the secret.

Sara relates the history of her sister's mental illness from her first psychotic episode, which occurred while she was doing an internship in Seattle after graduating from college, to her hospitalization and treatment in Chicago, where she was diagnosed with bipolar disease.

Yet, even as a child, Sara says, her sister had what she calls "dramatic moments"—at the age of two, driving the family car; trying to smoke a cigarette and inadvertently setting her parents' mattress on fire, and later, hosing down the neighbor kids all dressed up for a birthday party she wasn't invited to.

As part of assessing her sister's condition, the Chicago doctor asked her mother if there was a history of mental illness in the family. She told the doctor that her husband's mother was bipolar, but there was no mention that her husband may not have been the natural father.

Even now, Sara can't understand her mother's answer.

"My dad had been dead about four years at this time. Why, why, why would she let everybody believe that my dad's mother was bipolar? She could have said something about my dad might not be my dad. But she wanted us to believe he was our dad. Or maybe she didn't even know."

Was it shame that kept her mother quiet? Had she been told, like so many infertile couples receiving AID treatment in the early years, not to tell anyone? Or did she truly believe that her daughter's father was her father and not a sperm donor?

Sara puts her arm over her head and touches her forehead.

"Anyway, my sister committed suicide years later. She didn't leave a note."

In the aftermath of her sister's suicide, Sara is left trying to understand why her sister killed herself. She can only guess.

"About a year and a half before my mother died, she got dementia. I just don't think my sister could face that my mom was going to die."

A few weeks before she committed suicide, her sister told their mother's caretaker that she "can't imagine living without my mom around."

"You know the natural order of things is that our parents predecease us," the caretaker replied.

Another factor that might have contributed to her suicide was her divorce after twenty-five years of marriage. Maybe the impending death of her mom was one more loss she couldn't bear. Sara will never know.

"Bonus Family"

Sara shifts the conversation to the other half-siblings and what they inherited from their mutual sperm donor. Due to their frequent Zoom meetings and annual get-togethers, Sara, an early half-sibling, is conversant with many of their medical histories. Her recitation of their medical conditions shows the risks that were inherent in sperm donations before sperm banks and vetting.

There are half-siblings with mental illness, as well as autoimmune diseases. The sperm donor's mother had bipolar disease, and his sister died as a young adult from lupus, an autoimmune disease. One of the half-siblings has lupus, and as previously mentioned, Sara suffers from rheumatoid arthritis.

In the early experimental days of AID, donors weren't vetted, except for blood type. Today's vetting process screens for genetic diseases and mental illness, which would most likely have eliminated the half-siblings' donor. However, even today, sperm donation industry isn't regulated. And donors sometimes lie.

While the half-siblings may have inherited specific medical problems from their biological father, they also inherited his superior intellect and his musical ability. Several of the half-siblings are musicians and/ or music teachers.

Sara makes a point of telling me that she and her sister also have their biological dad's eyes. And that she and the "detective" half-sibling look alike, expressing the comfort of seeing and knowing your tribe reflected back at you.

After the interview, she emails me a photo of her and the half-sibling "detective," taken when he and his family visited Sara. Sara and her half-brother sit side by side on a couch smiling. It's striking how much they look like brother and sister.

When I ask her if she's told anyone in her extended family about the sperm donor and her multiple half-siblings, she says no.

"I don't think I want to tell them. It would just open up a whole can of worms."

Is her reluctance to tell family members concerned with the difficult question that still plagues her, and she can't answer with any certainty: What her mother knew or didn't know?

But she finds consolation in her relationships with her half-siblings, who she considers her "bonus family," even though her friends have always been and remain her main support.

"One of my biggest griefs in my life has nothing to do with this. My housemate, my friend, suddenly died in January 2021. He was a part of my life every single day for over five years. Then he was gone. It was very difficult for me. But I have my friends and my cats. They're the ones in my life."

As to the sperm donor who gave her life and her mother, she says, "I'm grateful to him, because I wouldn't be here. When my mom was dying, I said to her, 'thank you, mom. None of us would be here without you.'"

* * *

Like Robin, Sara is extremely helpful, emailing me annotated excerpts from the Artificial Insemination dissertation from her friend, information about the half-siblings and the family she grew up with, as well as other material that broadens my understanding of AID. She also facilitates an interview with another half-sibling.

A few weeks after our interview, Sara sends me additional information about her family as well as information she gathered from a phone call with one of the half-siblings. It's obvious she's been ruminating about the interview, which seems to have opened a door into her past, resurrecting things she thought had been buried.

At the end of her email, she says, "In looking back on it, I really think that my interview with you was therapeutic for me."

I'm pleased with her reaction. But, again, ticking at the back of my mind is the duty of care I feel toward her and the other interviewees—to honor their stories as if they were my own.

CHAPTER 21

———

A Family Trauma Unleashes a Secret
Tom (born 1974)

ROBIN EMAILS ME ABOUT TOM, ONE OF THE YOUNGER HALF-SIBLINGS WHO'S new to the group. In her beautifully discreet way, she says, "I'm not sure if he's exactly what you're looking for. But it's quite a story. In the end, it is about how some secrets can almost destroy a person. He says feel free to contact him."

I read Tom's email to Robin. His story is exactly what I'm looking for.

Within six months, he's experienced two horrific traumas.

Touched by his bravery and his willingness to go down a difficult and painful path with a relative stranger, I contact him immediately and set up a Zoom meeting.

He boldly states in his reply why he wants his story told.

"We are trying to take the shame out of it and stop the secrets, as there is only one person who deserves any shame."

Two things strike me about Tom: his resemblance to his donor father and his passionate mission to help others.

Before we begin the interview, he reassures me that it's okay to probe what must be a deep wound for him.

"I'm new to this," he explains. "But you don't have to worry about triggering me. It's something that's on my mind every day. Talking about it doesn't really bother me."

As a high school psychologist, I realize Tom is still actively processing what he calls "a messed-up situation." I also realize that he's probably skilled at this job that he loves.

"Messed-up situation" doesn't adequately describe the two emotional tsunamis that hit him in 2021. One in January and one in July. One of which was criminal.

A year later, he's still reeling from these assaults to his sense of self.

When I give him a thumbnail version of my own search for identity, his one-sentence description perfectly sums up the core of these discovery stories: "Who am I?"

I Never Felt I Belonged

As in so many of these misattributed parentage stories, Tom never felt he belonged, though he didn't have any inkling that his father wasn't his birth father.

"I would look at my two sisters. How are we related? We didn't look alike. We had different noses. We were different in so many ways. And I didn't resemble any of my dad's family. More my mom's side," he says. "I always struggled with who I was."

When Tom talks about his dad in more detail, he stops calling him dad, and refers to him by his given name, Jim. That's how deep his loathing goes for the man who raised him.

"I don't call him dad anymore," Tom says. "Because of his actions, he's forfeited his parental rights."

For the rest of the interview, Tom will refer to him as Jim.

Tom describes his relationship with Jim as one based on fear.

"I spent most of my younger life in fear of him. He wasn't physically abusive. He just wasn't emotionally available. I definitely got hit. But that wasn't uncommon back then. And I got yelled at a lot. In high school I hated him."

Jim never showed any interest in Tom, never attended his baseball games. He just sat on the couch and read the newspaper. Did his indifference come from not knowing definitively whether Tom was his biological son?

Tom admits that in high school he hung with the wrong crowd and got into trouble, getting drunk and high regularly. Instead of being suspended, he was forced to enroll in an alcohol prevention program, which proved to be a turning point for him. At one of the meetings, he talked to a dad whose alcoholic father had abused him. The man's story gave Tom insight into Jim and prompted him to forge a better relationship.

"I kinda forgave him and looked for ways to bond with him. He was into hunting, so at sixteen, I began hunting with him. We had fun and we bonded. But at some point, I realized I don't really like doing this. So, I started not shooting deer that walked by. The last one I shot, a big buck, that was when I said, 'I'm done.'"

He takes a deep breath, letting go of that memory. But the words, *I'm done* reverberate with another meaning that has nothing to do with hunting.

"That was right before the pandemic. And then, and then, this horrible thing with my daughter came out."

It Just Seemed So Horrific, I Couldn't Imagine That It Was True

Tom's daughter's devastating revelation began with a classroom activity related to the #MeToo Movement and Erin's law.

Erin's law is named after Erin Merryn, who was raped and molested by a neighbor and a family member for six and a half years. In her senior year in high school, she began a crusade to end the silence and shame around sexual abuse.

Mandated in most states, Erin's law requires that sexual abuse prevention education be taught to students in school every year.

The key component of Erin's law is that "all public schools should implement a child abuse prevention program with students in grades Pre-Kindergarten through 5th grade."[96]

Because of COVID restrictions, his daughter's class was being conducted remotely on Zoom. The class was discussing a character in a book who was abused. When one of the students asked, "Why wouldn't they just come forward and tell somebody?" Tom's daughter, who was thirteen at the time, said, "She probably dropped hints, and nobody picked up on it."

The teacher immediately sensed that something wasn't quite right with Tom's daughter. She wisely took his daughter aside and opened a private room in Zoom to talk with her.

Rather than ask if she'd been abused, the teacher asked if she had any younger cousins who might be in danger. And because his daughter didn't want anything to happen to them, she told the teacher that she'd been sexually abused by her grandfather, Tom's father, Jim.

Tom says he doesn't know if that's exactly how it came out. But he does know that the reason his daughter spoke up was because she didn't want anything to happen to her cousins.

Even after his daughter told her teacher, who then reported it to the principal, she didn't tell her parents what had occurred. The first time they learned that there was a problem with their daughter was a call from her school that the Department of Children and Family Services (DCFS) would be visiting them.

"We didn't know why. And she wouldn't tell us," Tom says.

After a sleepless night, they contacted the school to find out why DCFS would be coming to their house. The principal said it was something to do with Jim. Then he mentioned the sexual abuse.

"When he told us about the abuse, even then I wasn't sure that it was true. It just seemed so horrific. I couldn't imagine that it was true," Tom states.

After Tom and his wife were informed, the school counselor called the Child Advocacy Center to get their daughter's interview scheduled as quickly as possible, so that she didn't have to tell the story twice, which would have added to her trauma. The Child Advocacy Center works in concert with DCFS and law enforcement. The interview was taped and played for the DCFS worker.

Tom explains that when it's a criminal matter the police detectives override DCFS.

"After the police detective interviewed my daughter, he said to my wife and me, 'This absolutely happened. I've been doing this a long time and it happened.' That was a shock to me. At the time, I still had feelings for Jim."

He rubs his eye.

"It was very confusing."

Eventually, his daughter started to tell him and his wife some of the things Jim had done. Shockingly, the abuse had been going on as far back as his daughter could remember. She has no memory of it not happening. The only time it stopped was when she had a spinal fusion.

To keep her quiet, her grandfather had warned her if anybody found out, her dad wouldn't have a father and her grandmother wouldn't have a husband. His daughter lived in fear of ruining everyone's life. Jim had psychologically manipulated his granddaughter into submission and secrecy.

"The abuse happened in my parent's basement. My kids would spend the night there all the time. Built-in babysitters. We always thought, great, we're safe," he says with disgust.

As the investigation unfolded, it was discovered that Jim had abused other young girls besides his granddaughter. When the abuse came out, his older sister's friend came forward. She'd also been abused by Jim. He would take Tom's sister and her friend to the basement and take turns molesting them when they were five years old. His sister has no memory of the actual molestation. She only remembers not wanting to go to the basement. She was worried he was going to touch her.

After Tom's daughter revealed the abuse, she told her parents that one of her biggest fears was that if she wasn't believed, she'd lose her aunts and grandmother. They assured her that she was believed.

Angry and confused, Tom desperately wanted to get justice for his daughter, as well as protect her going forward. But he wasn't sure how. So, when the police suggested he go undercover to get Jim to admit what he'd done, he didn't hesitate.

"I went undercover for her," Tom says.

But at the back of his mind, simmering away, was a disturbing thought. How could he be related to someone who could do this—to someone the authorities believed was a pedophile?

I Thought She Was Sexually Exploring

The police instructed Tom what to say to get Jim to admit to the abuse. Because it's a technique that the police use and because Tom doesn't want to provide a manual for sexual abusers to exploit, he doesn't reveal exactly what he said. But he does say that he had to relate to Jim the details of what he'd done to his daughter, which was extremely disturbing for him.

"It got to the point where I just couldn't say anymore. It was so upsetting to me. But I was able to get him to admit on tape to a lot of the acts he'd done."

Tom pauses, then elaborates.

"Jim wanted to know how I knew about it. I said my daughter had told us."

Trying to understand the intense interaction between the two men, and Jim's reaction, I ask if he was remorseful or shocked.

Tom's answer stuns me.

"He said, 'I know this doesn't really matter. But I am sorry.' Then he went on to say that he knows my mom is going to divorce him. It's all about him. That's when I confronted him. 'How could you possibly do that? I can't even wrap my mind around it.'"

Jim responded, "I thought she was sexually exploring."

Angry and appalled, Tom explains how he had to hold himself together.

"I couldn't really say a whole lot, because I'm trying to get him to admit what he did."

With Jim's confession and Tom's daughter's interview, the police had enough evidence. The next day they arrested Jim and put him in jail. Tom and his wife were instructed not to tell anyone.

The first time they went to court, Jim stared Tom up and down.

"There's no remorse," Tom says disgusted. "He told my mom that I betrayed him. She lost it on him."

His mom filed for divorce and froze her husband's assets. Without any assets, he couldn't post bail. At the time of the interview, Jim had been in jail for a year. He'd yet to take a plea.

Since Jim's arrest, Tom's wife insisted that they go to every court appearance.

"When he's in court, we're in court," she told Tom. She wants the judge to see them there, so he puts a face to the crime.

Tom says his mom feels guilty. There were signs she thinks that she missed. Once when she confronted him about something not being right, he said, "How could you say that about me?" And she backed off, doubting her own judgment.

With Jim in jail awaiting trial, Tom continued to be haunted by what Jim had done to his daughter. How could he be related to this man? What was lurking in his genes? He worried about his son as well. He hated the thought that he had this in his genetics.

As a high school psychologist, he sees the impact abuse has on children.

"I do this for a living. . . . I love children. I can't imagine doing anything to harm them. That's what I was struggling to understand," he says. "You can't be a good person and do that. You have to be a sociopath who doesn't care about anybody but yourself. I just needed to understand that he's a horrible person."

But the repercussions lingered.

"My daughter and I always had trouble getting along. She saw me as him. Maybe because I replicated some of his behavior. Like him, I'm quick to anger. I have some of his mannerisms. But after the abuse came out, our relationship worsened."

He admits that he wasn't as emotionally available to her as he needed to be.

Then during an emotional encounter between his mother and his wife, a second tsunami rocked Tom's world.

My First Reaction Was Relief

What began as a family vacation ended in the revelation of a long-buried family secret. Tom, his wife and two children, his mother, and one of his two sisters were vacationing in Louisville, Kentucky. In attempting to park on a congested street near their Vrbo vacation home, Tom became frustrated. After exchanging heated words with his wife, he parked the vehicle, then went inside the rental home. Needing to chill out, he went upstairs.

His wife apologized to his mother for Tom's behavior.

"I'm sorry he reacted that way. When he gets upset, he reminds me of his father."

"That's not his father," his mother blurted out.

Flabbergasted, his wife replied, "We have to get Tom."

His sister, who heard the stunning admission, said nothing.

After Tom came downstairs, his mother confessed that Jim wasn't his biological father. Even more shocking, she said that Tom and his sister (the one vacationing with them) were both donor conceived. Only the youngest sister was Jim's biological child, which was no surprise to anyone. That sister had already taken an Ancestry DNA test confirming she was her parents' biological child. Interestingly, when the donor-conceived sister told her parents that she also was going to take the test, they talked her out of it.

Although Tom was shaken to the core and desperately wanted to be alone to process the disturbing news, he didn't leave. Seeing how upset his mother was, he stayed and tried to comfort her.

"I was consoling her and saying it's fine. Why would you think this would bother me? Frankly, my first reaction was relief."

With the truth of his donor conception revealed, questions remained. Why had his parents turned to artificial insemination by donor if they were able to conceive one child naturally? And why had they kept it a secret?

His mother explained that they'd used AID because of Jim's low sperm count, as a result of childhood mumps. Technically, it was possible for him to father a child, which explains the paternity of the youngest daughter, but it was highly unlikely.

At the time of the procedure, Tom's mother was told that her husband's sperm was mixed with the donor sperm. So, it was never certain that Tom and his one sister weren't Jim's children. Although, Tom thinks Jim always knew he wasn't his son.

Mixing the husband's sperm with the donor's sperm was a common practice, even if the doctor believed there was little to no chance that the husband's sperm was viable. The reason the physician did this was if the couple thought the child might be the husband's, it would ensure the husband's commitment to the child. But, of course, that left the child in a genetic limbo if the donor conception was revealed.

As understandable as the reason for AID was, Tom questioned his mother's justification for keeping it a secret.

"My mom was worried that my youngest sister would feel different or left out. It doesn't make any sense to me. And she said that Jim didn't want it known that he wasn't our father. He thought we'd look at him differently."

Although Tom doesn't bear any ill will toward his mother, he doesn't accept her reasons for keeping the AID secret.

"I'm very protective of my mom because of everything she's been through. But it was a horrible thing, keeping that secret."

He believes that shame surrounding infertility was part of their decision to keep the secret.

"The people who had this procedure done at that time, probably felt there was something wrong with them, because they couldn't have kids. Let's keep the secret going. And then it just gets bigger and bigger. The longer you don't tell, the more serious it gets."

He also thinks that his mother and Jim never thought about DNA when they had the procedure done in 1973. Mentally, they were never prepared to be confronted with the truth of their two children's conception.

Tom's wife wasn't quite as understanding. Because of inherent medical issues, she feels that they should have known that he was donor conceived prior to their having children. Maybe if they'd known his medical history, they could have detected their daughter's scoliosis sooner.

One of the positives that came from the revelation is that Tom and his daughter's relationship improved. But she, too, felt the AID shouldn't have been kept a secret. She told her grandmother, "Don't you think that was something I needed to know?"

While Tom felt relief knowing Jim wasn't his biological father, he told me that he experienced complete identity diffusion.

An article in the online journal, *ThoughtCo*, explains that identity diffusion usually occurs during adolescence, when people are working to form their identities. By learning Jim wasn't his father, a major part of Tom's identity vanished, triggering an identity crisis. If he wasn't Jim's son, then whose son was he?[97]

Needless to say, the rest of the vacation was ruined. Once they got home, Tom and his sister immediately ordered 23andMe DNA kits.

The results showed that they had different donor fathers. His sister opted not to find her biological father. She didn't want to know. Tom did.

"I wanted to find him. I wanted to find out as much as I could about him," he says. "Because I always had this need to help others. I wondered if that's something I got from my biological father?"

Nothing could have prepared Tom for what he found when he went searching for his ghost father.

Where Do I Belong?

In seeking his mysterious sperm donor, before receiving his DNA test results, Tom first questioned his mother about the donor selection process. Unfortunately, she knew little to nothing about the donor. He wasn't vetted, other than his blood type. (Doctors and providers matched blood types so that a blood test couldn't eliminate Jim as the father.) The physician also tried to match religions between the donor and the mother. (Tom's mother is Jewish. Jim is not.) So, all he was able to learn from his mother was the donor's blood type and that he was Jewish.

Therefore, Tom's DNA results were the key to finding his biological father, but at first, they baffled him. They indicated that he had a slew of aunts and uncles. He wasn't sure how he was related to them, so he picked the person with whom he had the most centimorgans and contacted that person.

That person responded saying there was a designated person who handled these inquires. She asked if it would be alright if she gave that person Tom's information, which he agreed to.

When he spoke with the designated person, she was relieved that he already knew he was donor conceived and she didn't have to break the news to him. Then she told him the story of his donor who had died some years ago.

As the woman told him about his donor and his multiple half-siblings, his mind began to splinter.

"I didn't know how to feel. I wasn't horrified. Part of me thought it was kind of cool. I was probably more curious than anything. And I was still so relieved I wasn't related to Jim."

He says he's grateful to his donor.

"I don't know what his reasons were for donating for all those years, but at the end of the day if it wasn't for him, I'm not here. There's nothing but love from my perspective."

While he does think it was unethical to make donations, sometimes twice a week, over thirty years in a small area, he adds that nobody considered the repercussions then.

Surprisingly, or maybe not so surprising, he discovered that he attended the same high school as one of the half-siblings.

"She graduated a year ahead of me. We never crossed paths. We never dated, fortunately."

He's already told his kids they have to get tested before they marry. Just to make sure there's no accidental incest.

Still, Tom views his donor in a positive light, seeing him as wanting to help infertile couples have children. He now knows the source of his altruism.

Amid his enthusiasm in discovering his paternal legacy, Tom wanted to get a tattoo representing his experience. He emails me a photo of the proposed tattoo. It's a sparsely leafed tree whose bark is twisted. All along the bark's twists and turns are birds, flowers, and a butterfly. The tree's roots are exposed tendrils.

When he told his wife about the tattoo, she said, "Why would you want a tattoo that represented your betrayal? Why would you want to signify that?"

He rethought the tattoo and was depressed for about a day, then abandoned the idea of the tattoo.

"I didn't really think about it that way. She was right. It was a betrayal."

No More Secrets

After a tumultuous 2021, in the summer of 2022, Tom met some of his half-siblings at the annual BBQ and pool party. While he thought that they were a nice group of people and felt a connection with them, he says he doesn't necessarily consider them his family.

"One thing I have learned is DNA doesn't really mean anything. . . . It really comes down to who is there for you when you need it, and who has your back."

After reflecting on the whole experience, he doesn't think the discovery has changed his sense of self.

"I look at this and think, I am who I am. And I was who I was before. What I've been through from the past until now shaped me. This is just part of that."

A year later, I write to him and ask for an update on Jim. The update is bittersweet. He got twenty years, which he will have to serve eighty-five percent of, so a minimum of seventeen years.

"But there really is no justice," Tom writes. "The devastation to my daughter and the entire family is insurmountable, and there is not enough justice in the world to rectify that. However, most victims don't get to see their abusers prosecuted, which we are grateful she was able to do."

He adds, "You know, my family's big on keeping secrets. But that's something we're not doing anymore."

CHAPTER 22

An Unbreakable Family
Ellen (born 1974)

"HOW DID YOUR PARENTS HAVE YOU?"

That was the awkward question people often asked Ellen when they found out her dad was a paraplegic. And if they didn't ask it, she knew they were thinking it. To her, it was a no-brainer. Her parents just did. Her dad was her dad. They were a family. She had no reason to think they weren't.

And when people commented that she looked Jewish, she sluffed it off. She knew her heritage. Her mom was Polish; her father was Swedish, German, and Irish. They were devout Catholics.

Then in July 2022, her sister-in-law gifted her and her brother 23andMe DNA kits. They did it for fun.

"We had no idea what was to come," Ellen says.

*   *   *

Ellen perches on a brown leather couch. Her open computer rests beside her. It's where she keeps her notes and the chronology of her life-changing journey. There's a preciseness about her, probably tied to her profession as a researcher and a college professor of writing and literature.

She holds a yellow pencil in her hand as if ready to jot down a note or stress a point. I imagine her giving a course lecture or encouraging a student.

"I have so many pieces of this puzzle that are not only difficult to fit together but to wrap my mind around," she says.

She's in the early throes of her donor-conceived discovery. Her vulnerability draws me into her narrative. With the exception of Tom, the other interviewees had the benefit of time to process and heal their psychic trauma.

Although Ellen's my daughter's age, I feel an instant rapport with her. Maybe it's because we're both college professors. At least I once was. Maybe it's because I admire her wanting to teach African American Literature at a Florida state college, where restrictions have been put on the curriculum, well aware of the taboo of a white woman teaching this class. Maybe it's that she asks me questions about *White Like Her*.

As we travel deeper into the interview, we begin to bond in a way I rarely experienced with the other interviewees.

Then it hits me. I've connected with a member of my tribe—a professor, a writer and researcher, and a woman who's had her life upended like mine was.

It's also our shared vulnerability. Ellen's discovery is barely one year old. And my husband of fifty-five years has just been diagnosed with a life-threatening illness. We're reaching across cyberspace to connect on the deepest human level where grief dwells and only another grief-stricken person can understand. And isn't that what these stories are about?

Unbreakable Family

"I grew up with a very profound sense of advocacy for the disabled," Ellen says, explaining how her father's war injury affected their family life and shaped her sense of self.

In 1967, at the age of nineteen, her father was severely injured in combat during the Vietnam War, leaving him a paraplegic.

"He was proud of being a Marine, but because his sacrifice wasn't honored, he was shrouded in shame and stigmatized," Ellen says. "My dad 'wore his scars' because he spent the rest of his life in a wheelchair and endured dozens of surgeries."

While her father was confined to a wheelchair, he wasn't defined by it.

He became a wheelchair athlete, who was very active in wheelchair Olympics, tennis, and basketball. He also was an artist, mainly a photographer and a painter.

When Ellen was five years old, the family moved from wintry South Bend, Indiana (where she and her brother were born), to summery Florida.

"The snow was just impossible for my father to get around in," explains Ellen.

Their Florida home was more than a home, it was the family's refuge, a safe harbor, and a quasi-hospital for her father—a place that forged Ellen's notion of family.

When Ellen was in middle school, her father went into end-stage renal failure. Her mother became proficient at in-home dialysis and converted her sewing room into a dialysis room. In 1999, Ellen's mother donated one of her kidneys to her husband, demonstrating her deep love for him.

Even the family's summer pilgrimage north to South Bend, Indiana, to visit her father's parents, Grammie and Grampie, as she fondly refers to them, only added to their unbreakable family bond.

So, when people learned that her father was confined to a wheelchair and questioned Ellen whether he was her father, the question bordered on insulting. The mere suggestion was emasculating to her father, this proud Marine. Besides, she'd studied her dad's photos and saw their similarities.

"I would say, 'oh, I have his pale skin and shape of face. His hair was kinda of wavy, like mine.' I looked for things like that."

23andMe and 1,500 Other Relatives

"We all thought it would be fun," Ellen laughs, referring to the 23andMe DNA kits her sister-in-law bought her and her brother. "I hear people say that all the time. It's just for fun."

Ancestry especially touts the fun inherent in discovering one's long-lost ancestors who've done incredible things and are waiting in the DNA wings to be discovered. The ads suggest the harmlessness of the discoveries that are as benign as finding out you weren't Irish, but German. Break out the lederhosen and brats.

But what began for Ellen and her brother as a bit of fun, upended her sense of self, making her doubt the foundation of her family.

Her brother received his results first. Excited, he texted Ellen a screenshot, which showed a wheel with two colors, a near even split:

51 percent Eastern European (Poland, Ukraine, plus 18 regions).

48.7 percent Ashkenazi Jewish.

Below the image he wrote: THERE IS NOTHING FROM SWEDEN, GERMANY, OR IRELAND (their father's ethnicity).

OMG, Ellen replied twice.

Her brother told her he had some theories about where the Swedish, German, and Irish went, which he didn't share with her.

What Ellen didn't know, because her brother had made his results public, was he'd already been contacted by one of their donor-conceived half-siblings, probably the woman who'd taken on the role of "ambassador" for this unusual familial group. She revealed the name of their sperm donor. Since Ellen hadn't received her results yet, he decided to withhold that information until she did.

Twelve days later, Ellen got her results:

50 percent Ashkenazi Jewish
48.5 percent Eastern European
1.5 percent Northwestern European

Her reaction was one of utter disbelief and confusion.

"I was lost. I didn't understand how I could be 50 percent Ashkenazi Jewish."

Even more perplexing, the results confirmed that she and her brother were full siblings, meaning they had the same mother and father. Considering that their mother was of Polish heritage (accounting for the high percentage of Eastern European DNA), and that neither of their parents were Jewish, Ellen concluded that the man who raised them wasn't their biological father.

Her mind swirled with uncomfortable scenarios: *Did their mom get pregnant by someone else? Maybe someone in the family?*

Several days later, Ellen's brother called her and asked if she was someplace where she could talk?

"He said that we have 1500 relatives, the maximum number on 23andMe. 'That's crazy,' I said. 'There's just no way.'"

To help her accept this new reality, he told her to make her profile public, so she could compare their profiles. Looking at the near identical profiles, and the matches with their biological siblings, she still didn't believe it.

"I told my brother this is ridiculous. This is junk. If you want to talk to those people, don't involve me. I think this is a scam."

Then he sent her a photo of their donor father.

When she saw the photo, she was astounded.

"I was like, that's my brother."

That same day, the half-siblings' "ambassador" sent Ellen a welcome letter:

Hi Ellen!
Welcome to 23andMe! You're probably pretty surprised to be on this list.
Just like your brother was, but we welcome you with open arms. I know this
all must be confusing, but feel free to contact me if you have any questions
at (XXX) XXX-XXXX, and I'll be happy to share any information that
I have. I've talked with your brother quite a bit and I've enjoyed getting to
know him. I'm sure he can fill you in on many of the details, and I can
explain things further if you'd like. Sincerely, XX

After reading the letter, Ellen thought, *Who is this nut job?*

"I was just baffled and frozen and confused. I needed more confirmation. So, I went into full-blown research mode, verifying that the
Chicago fertility clinic existed, who the clinic's director was, and the
research he did into infertility." *Okay, this is real.* Ellen thought.

"But I still didn't want to believe it."

Her brother suggested that they convince their mother to take a
23andMe DNA test, but not to tell her their real motive.

"At that point, we were starting to wonder if our mom was our
mom. Maybe she had a surrogate."

She takes in a deep breath.

"I completely lost who I was. I was shattered. I didn't understand how
I could be 50 percent Ashkenazi Jewish. I just couldn't understand it."

It Was Like a Death

Still wanting complete confirmation, Ellen contacted her first cousin on
her dad's side, who she's very close to, and confided in her.

"'Will you please, please take a 23andMe test?'" she begged her
cousin.

"'And please don't tell anyone.' I was still having doubts. My main concern was my dad wasn't my dad."

Her cousin immediately got a kit and sent it in. Ellen continued to speculate, leaning more towards doubting than believing, maybe hoping that her and her brother's DNA results were wrong.

While waiting for her cousin's DNA results, Ellen decided to contact the half-siblings' "ambassador." Their conversation lasted five hours and was informative and wonderful, though she remained skeptical. Was she still holding out hope that her paternal cousin's DNA would prove the 23andMe results wrong?

Ellen also sought help through psychotherapy once a week, sometimes twice a week.

"Thank goodness I had a therapist who as a child had experienced not knowing who her biological mother was," she says. "There are more people than I realized who don't know who their biological parents are."

About a month later, her cousin called with her DNA results, and they compared their reports.

Her cousin said, "I'm doing what you said. But where are you?"

In her cousin's 1500 relative matches, none matched Ellen. She had her confirmation. Her father wasn't her biological father.

"My heart just shattered. I was sobbing. All this time I was thinking, I know my dad's parents are my grandparents. They were so wonderful. They loved us so much."

Ellen begins to cry.

"When we'd arrive from Florida, my grandmother would be waiting, standing there with the door open. We weren't even in the door, and she'd squeeze us and hold us."

She rubs at her tears.

"I've never been hugged so hard in my life. We had such wonderful grandparents. I mean, I had grandparents who loved us so much."

Unexpectedly, her memory triggers one of my own—a sharp and poignant memory of my aged mother standing at the front door of our family home, watching my husband and I drive away after one of our visits. I remember thinking this might be the last time I see my mother in this life.

Ellen cuts into my thoughts.

"At that moment, there was no joy. It was loss. It was like a death."

Her cousin tried to console her.

"Ellen, this doesn't change anything. Your dad is still your dad. We're still family."

"And I thought to myself, *like hell it doesn't change anything*. All I could think about was, *I hope nobody else knows*. I begged her not to tell anyone."

Ellen puts her hands under her glasses and blots at her tears, then she grabs a tissue.

"And so, then I knew. That was hard."

She takes a moment before continuing.

"It was like I was stepping up a ladder and I just didn't know what was at the top. I know there's going to be some answer there. But maybe as obscure as the clouds in the sky. I didn't know."

What Did My Mom Know?

Even though Ellen now accepted her father wasn't her biological father, and that she had a group of half-siblings, serious questions dogged her that only her mother could answer. How did this happen? Why weren't she and her brother told?

She wanted to have a face-to-face conversation with her mother, but her plan to confront her was delayed by unforeseen life events: two hurricanes, her mother's move from the family home to a retirement community, and a hectic Christmas holiday. Then the unthinkable happened. On March 3, 2023, Ellen was in a very serious car accident and sustained injuries.

Burdened with the secret she'd been keeping for six months; she decided she couldn't wait any longer. She called her mother.

She began the conversation very gently and lovingly, asking her mother if she'd looked at her 23andMe results. She replied that she'd only briefly glanced at them. Eventually, she eased into telling her about the half-siblings.

"I shared the good stuff. Meeting them on the Zoom call. How warm and friendly they were. I was just so relieved that I was no longer keeping the secret."

I ask her what her mother's reaction was.

"She was surprised, but she listened. Then she started talking. But she never said your dad isn't your dad. Never."

Ellen learned that her mother had miscarried twice before having her and her brother. Since her mother was O negative, her pregnancies were considered high risk. Not wanting to risk another miscarriage, her mother and father sought the services of a Chicago fertility clinic.

They filled out forms and pictures of them were taken. Her mother was in one room, her father in another. The procedure was performed when her mother was ovulating.

"My mother told me she had the procedure done twice. Though she knew donor sperm was an option, she told my dad absolutely not. She couldn't have someone else's children. She was under the impression that the doctor used my dad's sperm. It's very likely that's what she was told," Ellen explains.

Now faced with the reality that a sperm donor was used; her mother thinks her husband made a decision she wasn't aware of and hadn't agreed to.

"I know my dad," Ellen says. "If my mom said no, he had the final decision. That could have been what happened."

If her father had made an executive decision going against his wife's wishes, Ellen will never know. He died in 2008.

Exploring the possibility that her mother might not have been totally deceived, she asked her mother if her dad went with her every time.

"My mom said, 'Yeah, your dad and I both went.' But later on, she told me she went by herself and dad stayed in the car."

Which raises another question: Was frozen sperm used in the early 1970s? When Ellen asked the half-siblings, they insisted that frozen sperm wasn't used.

Her mother has a distinct memory of bringing a vial to the clinic, which she assumed was her husband's frozen sperm.

Ellen wonders what the real story is?

Another theory Ellen thinks is possible is that the insemination was so traumatic for her mother she wanted to believe it was her husband's sperm. Since the records are missing, she can't know the details of her mother's procedure.

However, unlike some of the other half-siblings, Ellen is not convinced that a fire destroyed the records. She combed through newspaper articles during that time period and didn't find any mention of a fire in that location. Ellen's mother also stated that the clinic was in a large building and that a fire would have destroyed other businesses, as well.

"My mother and I talked for hours. I was relieved, but I was still very depressed," she says.

Her late-night research scrolling databases about AID and the early pioneers left her unsettled. Had the doctors misled her mother?

"I'm a radical feminist," Ellen states. "I was so disgusted by the fertility treatment that was managed by men back then. Using medical students, all white. It just makes me sick sometimes thinking about it.

"But then when I think about my parents and what they had to go through to have me and my brother, I'm appreciative that the doctors were able to do that for them. I've come to understand how my parents were situated in history in the 1970s. The pressure they were under. They were Catholic from devout Catholic families. You got married and had babies right away. I try to remember that. But at the same time, we have half-siblings who could have married and had babies. I have a hard time with the decision the donor made to donate for all those years."

Supporting Ellen's assessment, Ann Fessler, the author of *The Girls*

Who Went Away, points out that: "Married couples who were not raising children seemed odd in the prenatal environment of the 1950s and 1960s. The desire to parent and to conform to the normal social and family expectations of the times, imposed substantial strain on couples who could not conceive."[98]

For Ellen's mother, it's still sinking in.

"She has a lot of questions about what happened. What my dad knew, but maybe didn't tell her? Or what the doctors did and didn't tell her or my dad? It's a sensitive topic for her."

The sad part for Ellen is not knowing with certainty what her mom knew or believed to be the truth. Was a donor sperm used without her knowledge? Or if she knew, has she buried the secret so deep that she refuses to admit it?

In pondering whether her mother knew about the sperm donor, Ellen recalls her mom's worries about the paternal side of the family's medical history, which might hold an answer for her.

"My mom would have told me if she knew about the donor. Seeing what I went through, she would have told me."

I Felt Like a Liar

In July 2022, two months before Ellen discovered her father wasn't her biological father, wiping all genetic connection to her paternal side, she made the momentous decision to have a total hysterectomy. One of the factors putting her at high risk for cancer was her previous paternal medical history. She was forty-eight years old.

Cancer snakes through the family tree of the father who raised her. Both paternal grandparents had breast cancer. There also is a history of cervical and ovarian cancer.

"My mom always told me to make sure I tell my OB/GYN about Grammie and Grampie's breast cancer," Ellen explains.

It took her three years to make that radical medical decision, involving meeting multiple times with her OB/GYN, an oncologist, and a geneticist. Each of them took extensive medical histories. Her father's side seemed to draw their attention the most. Both the oncologist and OB/GYN asked if she was Jewish.

She told them no.

About four months after her discovery, when she made her annual appointment at a breast cancer clinic, the realization that her paternal medical history was gone, with nothing to replace it, is when everything really hit her.

"I broke down sobbing. My paternal medical history was all wrong. It felt like half of my life was a lie. I felt like a liar, a fraud."

Now she had the arduous and emotional task of correcting her paternal medical history. When she told her OB/GYN that she'd been right, that she was 50 percent Ashkenazi Jewish, her doctor said, "I knew all along you were Jewish."

She shared her 23andMe results showing all her half brothers and sisters and explained that her biological father was in the medical field. The doctor said, "See, I told you that you came from something good."

Prior to her appointment with her oncologist, she had to complete a new medical history. She had no relevant medical history other than what she'd learned from her half-siblings, which wasn't much. The sperm donor had Parkinson's disease and there was a history of mental illness and autoimmune disease on his side.

The nurse practitioner who saw her that day was stunned.

"In case she didn't believe me, I brought printed copies of my 23andMe report with all my half-siblings. I tried to hold back tears but couldn't. I don't know what's worse, a false-but-very-extensive medical history of who I thought were my biological paternal relatives. Or the unusual discovery of who they really were."

Again, Ellen repeats her belief that her mom probably didn't know about the sperm donor. "That's one of the reasons I think she feels so bad now."

Pilgrimage

As part of her healing process, Ellen attended the fourth annual get-together of the half-siblings hosted by the donor's natural daughter. Ellen is grateful to her for allowing them to come together and to be a family. When she met her half-siblings for the first time in person, she felt an instant connection.

"There was something freeing about the experience. I hadn't felt this happy in a very long time. It helps me feel proud. It helps me to heal. It helps me to have understanding."

Yet, she still struggles to express the two sides of herself—the Polish and the Jewish. It's a huge part of her identity that she doesn't know how to reconcile.

I tell her about Kara Rubinstein Deyerin, CEO of Right to Know and subject of Chapter 7, and what's she done to integrate her Jewish identity. I see the doubt in her eyes and say it's a process, knowing all too well how difficult it is and how it's ongoing.

Then she mentions her two sons. She shared their genetic makeup with them but cautioned her high school–aged son not to tell anyone. With the closed-mindedness of the Florida public school system and the atmosphere it breeds, she's concerned someone might treat him badly because he's Jewish

"It's very real. What's happening in Florida. It's very, very real. What I mean by that is the legislature telling us how to teach African American literature. It's mortifying. It's frightening."

But the question remains for Ellen, how does she move forward?

"I still want to know where those records are. I want to know what rights my mom had, what my mom can do to bring her some peace. At the end of the day, we have rights, too. To our medical history."

She pauses and smiles.

"I'm one of those research detectives like you."

Seeking solace, she reflects back on her trip to meet her half-siblings.

"When I was there, it was like a pilgrimage for me. As I move on with my life, after learning the truth about my biological father, memories and events sometimes trigger me. And there I am, left alone, sitting with the trauma. But now, I have half brothers and sisters that I can talk to."

CHAPTER 23

A Skewed Sense of Truth
Bridget

WHILE BRIDGET WAS DONOR-CONCEIVED, SHE ISN'T A HALF-SIBLING OF THE forty-nine-and-counting group. She had a decidedly different experience when she finally found her donor and his family.

It's important to recognize that not every donor-conceived offspring is welcomed by his or her donor and his family. It's an emotional risk donor-conceived people take when they search for their donors in their desire for identity and connection. There are many reasons men donate sperm, from monetary to altruistic.

Additionally, donors from earlier generations were promised anonymity, which adds another layer of complication for the donor-conceived person, as well as the donor. Having a donor-conceived person show up on the donor's doorstep can throw his life into chaos. And if the donor-conceived person is rejected, it can be devastating to them.

* * *

Bridget's dad used to sing to her "Brown-eyed Girl" by Van Morrison. While she loved that he celebrated her dark brown eyes, she often wondered where they came from. No one in the family had her dark eyes and dark hair. And no one in the family ever had a convincing answer.

"As a child, my sense of truth was always kind of skewed," Bridget says.

That perspective was never more evident than on Christmas eve, when her extended family gathered together. To this day, one of their family traditions is to take a group photograph of the children. In this large Irish family, the cousins line up on the staircase for the Christmas card photo.

Bridget says, "I remember looking at that Christmas photo and feeling like that Sesame Street song, 'One of These Things (Is Not Like the Other).'"

"I stuck out like a sore thumb. Both my parents are Irish Catholic. My mom is Irish and French. Everybody in the family pretty much has these beautiful blue eyes and are light featured. Here I am with these big brown eyes, darker features, and dark hair. I was different."

When she mentioned to her dad's sister that she didn't look like anyone in the family, her aunt said, "Oh, I think we have someone in the family who was Spanish Irish or Black Irish."

Bridget's parents said nothing.

Her mother always claimed that Bridget looked like her, and that her brother looked like their dad.

But the outside world saw Bridget and her brother differently. When they were children, people often pointed out how she and her brother looked nothing alike.

Bridget's sense of truth was also warped by her father's chronic illness, non-Hodgkin's lymphoma.

"You really didn't know what was going to happen from one moment to the next," Bridget explains, gesturing with her hands. "Everything was high stakes."

Each time her father would be hospitalized for complications related to his cancer; her mom would try to warn her and her brother that he might not make it through the surgery. Then, miraculously, he would.

"He was such a positive guy. He'd return from the hospital and say, 'I'm fine. I'm going to be okay now. I'll always be there for you.'"

Even when he was in hospice care at home and her mom was trying to prepare her and her brother for his death, Bridget still believed he'd make it. She'd been told to prepare for his death so many times, she thought he'd survive. But this time, he didn't.

He died when Bridget was eleven years old and in sixth grade.

"I'd seen him pull through so many times that his death was a real shock to me. I felt his absence. His death left a huge hole in my heart."

Three years later, Bridget received another shock that blindsided her and added to her grief. Compounding the loss of her beloved dad was the loss of her identity.

How Can You Not Know?

Bridget can only speculate why her mom decided to reveal the truth of her conception on this particular day.

"I think my mom kept that secret for my dad. She was holding on to it for him, because he really wanted to believe that we were his. But once he passed, there was no reason to keep it anymore."

Whatever her mom's reasons, what initiated the revelation was a neighbor saying to Bridget that she and her brother looked nothing alike, and that her brother looked so much like her dad.

"I came home really upset. I told my mom what the woman said. And it just burst out of her. She told me that I'd been artificially conceived. I was absolutely shocked. I was still grieving my dad. Then to find out that this man I was grieving wasn't my biological father felt like something else was taken from me. But at the same time, there was this weird sense of relief," Bridget says.

Now, she understood why she didn't look like anyone else in the family. The first thing she wanted to know was: What was she? What was her ethnicity?

"This is a question that has haunted me my whole life—my ethnicity."

"I have no idea," her mom told her. "It was completely anonymous."

"How can you not know?" Bridget said incredulously.

Her mother's answer baffled her.

"The doctor said that because we were Catholic, he didn't think we wanted to play God. So, he would pick a donor who looked like your father."

"Well, that clearly didn't happen," Bridget answered.

When she asked her mom if there was any paperwork, she said, "There's a good chance there wasn't any."

Wanting answers, Bridget urged her mom to call the fertility clinic where the procedure took place. She didn't call right away. When she did, the office manager practically laughed in her face when she asked about medical records and paperwork.

She was told that the treating doctor died a while ago, and if there was any paperwork, it was destroyed ten years from the time of treatment.

They were five years too late.

And what about her brother? Bridget wanted to know if he had the same donor.

Her mom told her no.

"That stuck with me. The way I took their using a different donor was they were disappointed with what they got the first time. That they wanted to make sure they had a donor who looked like my dad the second time," says Bridget. "Though my mom swears that's not true, for a long time, that's how I interpreted it."

In one fell swoop, Bridget lost her dad and part of her identity. And her brother was now her half-brother.

Not until Bridget was older would she learn the disturbing and misguided circumstances that necessitated her parents seeking a sperm donor.

Her parents were nineteen and engaged when her dad was diagnosed with cancer. His doctor cautioned him that chemotherapy occasionally causes infertility and that he should freeze his sperm.

Since they were devout Catholics, they sought spiritual guidance from their priest, who said it was against their religion to freeze sperm. So, he declined.

After completing chemotherapy, they tried to have a child, but couldn't conceive. As the doctor had predicted, the chemotherapy had rendered him sterile. The doctor suggested using a donor.

Before embarking on artificial insemination, her parents sought a priest's advice again—only this time, they went to a younger priest. They told the priest that they really wanted a family and needed to know if it was against their religion to use a donor.

"Are you going to raise the children Catholic?" the priest asked.

"Yes, of course," they answered.

"Then it doesn't matter," he said.

With the priest's blessing, they went forward with the artificial insemination by donor procedure.

When You're the Secret

Throughout high school, Bridget kept her donor conception a secret out of respect for her mother and her deceased father. But it took a toll on her.

"Holding a secret like that, it really messes with you," Bridget says. "Especially when you're the secret."

Once in college, she realized how much her ethnicity mattered. She felt she had to be more honest about who she was.

"When people asked what my ethnicity was, I'd say, 'I'm Irish and not sure about what else. I don't know my biological father.' I usually didn't say anything more."

Sometimes she'd elaborate to protect her mom.

"I'd say my dad couldn't have kids. I didn't want people to assume my mom had a kid with someone else."

But no matter how much she revealed to people, a part of her remained a blank space. Her uncertain ethnicity really became a problem after college, when she decided to pursue a career in the entertainment field in New York City. Her dark hair and dark eyes didn't match her very Irish first and last name.

"My first agent told me that I should change my name. Because it's very confusing to casting directors. She said, 'You have the most Irish name and casting directors are expecting a blond or a red-headed girl to walk in the room, and you walk in. It's very confusing.'"

At first, she resisted changing her name, thinking it would be a betrayal of her family. Then she reconsidered, wanting more control over her own narrative.

If Bridget was going to change her last name, it had to be meaningful. While taking an acting class in London, she bonded with a woman who became her mentor and dear friend. She credits this woman with setting her on the right path at a time in her life when she was running away from her feelings. After getting the woman's permission, she chose her name as her last name, which happened to match her appearance. Little did Bridget know that the derivation of the name reflected her true ethnicity.

The name change worked. She started to receive callbacks and was cast in Latina and Hispanic roles. Uneasy playing these roles, Bridget was always upfront about her identity, explaining that she was half Irish and she didn't know the other half. She questioned whether she was assuming an identity that wasn't hers.

"Even though the Hispanic and Latina community embraced me, I started to feel uneasy because I had no idea where I belonged."

When auditioning for a part, she always feared she'd be asked what she was. In the acting field, your identity, knowing who you are, walking on stage with confidence, is key. Which box did she check in an industry that prizes appearance? She could only check one box—Irish. Which would inevitably lead to the question: "Why don't you know your full ethnicity?"

A turning point in Bridget's career came when she took an acting class in New York. Everyone in the class had to perform in front of several casting directors, who would give them feedback about their performances.

Bridget decided to sing a song from *In the Heights*, a Tony award–winning musical set in a New York City Latino neighborhood. After her performance, one casting director, a white woman, said, "Honestly, I wasn't even paying attention to your song. Because the whole time you were singing, I was just thinking, is she white or is she Latina? I can't tell. Well, that was what I was thinking. And I can't legally ask you."

Bridget lost it.

"Well," she responded angrily, "I'm half Irish and I don't know who my biological father is, so I don't know what I am. What do you think a person like me should do in this business? Should I not play anything? Are there any characters who don't know who their fathers are?"

"I was pissed," Bridget adds. "That was one of the last straws."

At thirty, she stepped away from the theater industry for a while, went to massage therapy school, and bought a DNA test.

She wasn't specifically looking to find her donor. She just wanted to know her ethnicity. Maybe then, she felt she could return to the theater with confidence in who she was.

"I was going to finally put this to rest," Bridget says. "I took the test and my life forever changed."

Is This Really How My Story Ends?

Before opening her DNA test results, Bridget called her mom, who'd been supportive of her search to find her donor's ethnicity. However, her mom believed Bridget was Italian, not Latina.

The results confirmed what Bridget had always suspected, 63 percent of her DNA was from the Iberian Peninsula. Quickly, she looked up Iberian Peninsula and discovered that Andorra, Spain, and Portugal were the primary countries forming the Iberian Peninsula. Even though she didn't know yet which country her ancestors were from, she was thrilled. She'd been playing Hispanic and Latina roles for years and feeling guilty about it—not sure if she was a white girl masquerading as a Hispanic.

Her mom was in complete shock.

"The doctor lied to me," she said. "He was going to find an Irish guy who looked like your dad."

Disappointingly, Bridget's results didn't match with a donor or half-siblings. The closest paternal matches were second cousins.

However, one of the second cousins had posted a photo of herself on an ancestry site. Bridget clicked on it and saw a woman with her eyes. After a lifetime of feeling different from her family, finally she saw herself in this woman.

"I was blown away," Bridget says. "My whole life people complimented me on my eyes. And I always wondered where they came from."

Now she knew.

Bridget changed her mind about finding her biological father, so she messaged the paternal second cousin, explained that they were a second cousin match, and that she was donor conceived. The woman agreed to meet with her at a Cuban restaurant. Perhaps this woman would help her find her donor.

"Knowing my ethnicity wasn't enough. I wanted to know who my donor was. It was so powerful seeing my cousin's eyes. I wanted to see my donor's face."

When Bridget and her cousin met, she told her why she'd chosen a Cuban restaurant.

"I want you to know we're Cuban as hell," she said. Seeing the confused look on Bridget's face, she explained that the family was Cuban by way of Spain. Their family is from Havana.

Before Bridget relates how she discovered her donor's identity, she asks me not to put the information in the book because she wants to protect certain paternal family members.

Of course, I agree not to disclose her three-year journey to find her biological father. After I hear the details, I'm amazed at her tenacity. Three years is a long time to keep pursuing a ghost father.

"What drove you to keep looking for him?" I ask.

Her answer reveals the longing people with unknown parentage possess to know their tribe, to know where they come from. Whether they were adopted or donor conceived, identity is core to their existence as it is to everyone's.

"If you've never been without something, you don't understand what it's like to have it missing. It felt like my life was a mystery movie. I just wanted to know the ending. And I really thought to my core that I'm going to have a happy ending. Because my dad died already, it can't get any worse than that," Bridget says.

But that's not what happened.

In 2020, during the COVID lockdown, Bridget finally found her donor with the help of her roommate and friend. Surprisingly, her donor lived twenty minutes from her.

Excited to learn more about him, she typed his name into Facebook. His photo popped up. The shock of seeing the man who gave her life jolted her.

"I literally knocked over my chair. It was like looking at myself. It was genetic mirroring. Though I knew I'd found him, I still sought confirmation," Bridget says.

Once she'd confirmed that he was her biological father, she crafted a letter and emailed it to him. In the letter, she stated that she wasn't seeking anything except medical history, that she was engaged and needed the medical information for future children, and that she wanted to make a connection with him.

Three days later, she got an email from someone who said they worked for him.

Bridget smiles.

"From her name, I knew it was his sister—my aunt."

The aunt's letter was succinct, professional, and lacking in compassion and empathy. Her biological aunt confirmed that he'd donated sperm during that time period to pay for medical school, and that he also really wanted to help couples who couldn't have families.

Bridget scoffs at his supposed altruistic motive.

"No, he did it for the money. Can we please be real?"

What really wounded Bridget was not just the letter's coldness, but that he had no interest in a connection. The letter explained his view that donors remaining anonymous is the way it should be, and that technology has robbed people of well-deserved anonymity. The letter went on to say that all she needed to know was that Rheumatoid Arthritis runs in the family. It concluded with: "Happy to see that your parents had a healthy baby girl."

Understandably, compounded with all she had been through with her father's illness and early death, Bridget felt utterly rejected. In her subconscious, she always thought there was this paternal figure out there that would complete her.

According to Bridget, usually a donor rejects contact because they're married, and their partner feels threatened. Her donor is divorced. So, she was surprised by his reaction.

"Is this really how my story ends?" she questioned. "It felt like a tragedy."

It took months for her to come to terms with his rejection. However, not everyone in the family rejected her. Since connecting to her paternal family, she's become close to two second cousins who want to bring her into the family. But certain members of the family are against it.

The family Bridget grew up with had a radically different reaction when they learned from her Facebook posting that she was donor conceived.

"It changes nothing," her dad's closest brother said. "You're still family, whether it's in your blood or not."

Regarding her identity, even though Bridget now knows her ethnicity, she still feels a sense of not belonging.

"I mean, I'm 63 percent Cuban. But I grew up in complete white privilege. I never had the cultural experience of growing up in a Cuban household. But I've been trying to educate myself about Cuban history."

She finds that white people think she's white and Latino people think she's Latina. "Everybody sees what they want to see."

If people ask Bridget what she is, now she says I'm Cuban and Irish. Secure in her ethnicity, she's returned to the entertainment industry.

Recently she met a playwright who's also Cuban and Irish, and he said he calls himself Cubish.

"I'm going to start calling myself Cubish, because it kinda makes sense."

Not So Surprising Update

Weeks later, when we have our second interview, she tells me there's been a huge development.

"I have a half-sister."

Her enthusiasm is contagious. I'm really pleased for her.

The message came to her via 23andMe.

"Hi Bridget, So, I guess I'm your half-sister. My test results came this morning. I'd like to speak to you. I'd love to know if you know who our biological father is.

During their initial conversation, her half-sister drops a bomb—she's a twin.

"I now have a half-sister and a half-brother," Bridget says.

She suspects there are more half-siblings waiting in the wings.

"My donor is going to have to come to terms with all this."

Then she abruptly shifts gears, sharing her online dating experiences.

"When I tell someone I'm donor conceived, nine times out of ten, they have no idea what I'm talking about. Their usual response is: 'What is that?'"

EPILOGUE

CHAPTER 24

The Last Piece of My Racial Discovery Journey
What My Brother Knew

WHEN MY MOTHER DIED, I LOST MY BROTHER, MY ONLY SIBLING. NOT TO death, but to an angry silence so absolute we didn't speak for over six years. During that time, I made multiple public appearances and was often asked if I had siblings, and if they knew about my mother's racial secret.

I always gave the same sad answer.

"My brother and I are estranged. That's all I'm going to say."

Sometimes, I added, apologetically, "You know how it is with families."

No one ever asked why we were estranged. And if they had, I couldn't explain it to them. How do you summarize a lifetime of distance and misunderstandings, culminating in a severed relationship? Our mother had been the glue that held us together, however tenuously. Once she was gone, whatever bond we had disintegrated.

The silent years took a toll. In one fell swoop, as if a catastrophic event had occurred, my brother, his children, and grandchildren disappeared from my life. Family loss compounded. No more occasional phone calls or visits. No more Christmas or birthday cards.

As I traveled around the country lecturing, telling strangers about my mother's racial secret, I sometimes wondered if my brother knew about my book and our mixed-race heritage. If he hadn't read the book, surely someone told him about my appearance on *The Megyn Kelly Today Show*. I both welcomed and feared what he would say to me.

"You had no right to tell people about mom." Or "It's not true." Or maybe, "Tell me more about it."

All possibilities, all dependent on how he viewed what I'd revealed about our family. And how that revelation affected his sense of self.

After my appearance on *The Megyn Kelly Today Show*, I received an anonymous email, short and cruel. "You sold your family for 30 pieces of silver." Had my brother or one of his children sent it? I deleted it and moved on.

When I gave two separate talks in Ohio, near where we grew up, I worried he'd show up and cause a scene. My brother's temper was quick, sure, often beyond reason. Thankfully, he never came.

But he wasn't far from my thoughts, sometimes invading my dreams.

Journal Entry: April 15, 2018

Strange dream about my brother last night. I'm not sure where we were. He's holding a large manilla envelope. On the outside I see my father's printing and one of his doodles. But I can't read the words. My brother hands me the envelope. Inside are photos of mixed-race people. From the expression on my brother's face and the photos, I know he's bringing me a message that my father knew about our mother's mixed race. I'm surprised and grateful. In return for his gift, I'll give my brother the photos of his family that are stored in my basement. When I wake up, I'm sad. If only we could make peace with each other. Four years now we've been apart, with no communications.

Paging back one day in my journal to April 14, I read: ANNIVERSARIES ARE KILLERS.

Four years out, I was still mourning my mother who died on April 5, 2014. Grief has no expiration date.

Yet neither of us bridged the hurtful silence that had fallen between us.

Had we been closer, would it have mattered? I don't know. We were just too different. When I left home at twenty-one to marry, I never lived in Ohio again. My brother stayed. Over the years, we seldom saw each other, except for my occasional trips home. Even then, our time together was brief, peppered with kids and our parents. I can't remember ever talking to him alone about our lives or our childhood experiences—some heartwarming, some heartbreaking.

Our relationship had become so distant that when I learned in 1995 that our mother was passing as white, I didn't tell my brother, even though I felt he had a right to know his heritage. When I confronted my mother two years later about her racial secret, I asked her if I could tell my brother. She said no, vowing me to secrecy until after her death. Her insistence was so adamant, I agreed. I became complicit in her deception, carrying on the legacy of a racial secret. I often wondered why she didn't want him to know. Of course, I could have gone against her wishes, but I reasoned that it was her secret to tell.

Distance and time kept us apart, and an unwillingness to forgive the harsh words spoken to each other weeks after our mother's death. I thought I'd never see or speak to him again in this life, then a horrible thing happened.

*   *   *

On January 21, 2021, a tragedy brought us back together. When I saw my brother's phone number come up on my call log, I knew something was terribly wrong. I didn't hesitate; I answered.

His youngest daughter was dying. There'd been an accident. She was on life support. It didn't look good. I offered what little solace I could, but mostly I listened.

Over that long weekend, he and his wife sat by her bedside talking to her. He told me that if there was no change by Monday, they'd decided to take her off life support. It was tearing him up. In the halting way he spoke, struggling for words, I heard his immense sorrow.

I told him I thought it was the right decision. She had no brain activity. This vibrant woman wouldn't want to be kept alive on machines.

On Sunday night, she died and spared them that agonizing decision. I had my brother back, but at what cost?

Reading through my journal at that time, I'm startled by an entry I made on January 19, 2021, two days before my brother's call, the night of his daughter's accident:

> *I dreamed of my brother. I'm in a city with a few women. One collapses in the street. I go to her. Suddenly my brother appears and tries to pull me away. "You have to come with me," he says. I resist. "I have to help the woman," I plead. He answers, "It's about mom's money. Thousands of dollars." I agree to leave the woman. "Let's find somewhere we can talk," I suggest. We finally find a quiet restaurant. Then I wake up.*

I say nothing to my brother about my dream. Although, like me, he believes in premonitions and the unexplained—a legacy from our New Orleans mother and our grandmother, Camille, who had second sight.

During those difficult weeks after my niece's death, I finally learned whether my brother knew about our mother's racial secret.

My brother said he had suspicions.

"Do you remember when that relative visited?" he asked. "I can't remember his name. Since my stroke, my memory is shit."

He said of this unnamed relative, "Well, we went fishing together. And I thought maybe he was part Black."

The only male relative who ever visited us alone was my mother's half-brother Uncle Warren from my grandmother Camille's second marriage.

I don't dispute his suspicion, but I question it. When Uncle Warren visited, I was thirteen, and my brother was eight. Even if he'd thought he was part Black, his ethnicity could have come from his father. My grandmother Camille was as white as I was.

Although we'd reunited, I felt there was an elephant in the room. Rather than rehash what caused our rift, I said to my brother that if he was willing, we should just let the past go.

"Let's just move forward," I suggested. He agreed.

Even though we were speaking again, maybe because of the stroke, his voice was altered. He spoke slowly, choosing his words with care. He was no longer the gregarious fun-loving brother I once knew.

Sometimes, he'd hand the phone to his wife, as if talking exhausted him or he'd run out of things to say—once a man who loved to talk.

But I knew he was a ticking time bomb—a life-long smoker, over-weight, diabetic, and with a heart condition. I suggested he stop smoking. He listened, said nothing, and continued to smoke.

Our reunion would be short lived.

*   *   *

On July 28, 2022, a year and a half after our reconciliation, my brother suffered a massive brain bleed.

Though he survived, he was severely compromised. It was unclear if he would ever swallow, talk, or walk again. He was airlifted to University Hospital in Cleveland. But because of his other health issues, it took three hours in the ER to stabilize him, further compromising his condition.

Two weeks before his catastrophic brain bleed, I called him twice, asking him to call me. It was as if I knew. He didn't call me back. Finally, I texted his wife and asked her to have him call me. I wish I could remember what we talked about. If only I'd known that would be the last time, we would ever speak to each other—the last time I'd hear his voice.

The next four months were marked with glimmers of hope, and sometimes wanton neglect. He was shuffled around from a hospital then to a residential care facility, back to another hospital, and then another residential care facility. The revolving door of health care ruled by Medicare restrictions.

Intubated, on a ventilator, a feeding tube surgically implanted through his stomach (PEG surgery)—the doctors kept assuring my sister-in-law that he needed time to heal.

Every morning, my one question was: Is my brother still in this world?

Almost daily, I recorded his fluctuating condition as reported to me by my sister-in-law. If distance and time had eroded my relationship with my brother, my sister-in-law and I had no relationship to erode.

Now we were deeply rooted, offering each other comfort.

While my brother struggled to live, I continued to write this book. I'd like to say it was cathartic. It wasn't. Transcribing these stories of parental secrets, hidden identities, and shattered families trying to heal was a struggle. Every story intensified my feelings of loss.

There were days I couldn't write, when the pain of my brother's illness spilled into the stories, or the pain of the stories spilled into my life, reinforcing my feelings of helplessness and loss. Why hadn't we tried sooner to reconnect, to mend what was broken?

After listening to Brad Ewell's story from Chapter 13, I wrote:

> *I'm finding it hard transcribing Brad Ewell's interview, listening a second time to the trauma of his story, the way people's lives spin out, and the collateral damage it causes. His story pulls me under to a dark place I fear to go, where family ties erode or break, seldom mended, and never the same.*

In the beginning of October, I began to accept that my brother may never get better, that he might live the rest of his life severely compromised—a half-life. He would hate that.

At Thanksgiving, he showed signs of recovery. In frustration, he'd taken out his trach (a common thing for intubated patients to do), and surprisingly, he was able to breathe on his own. He also was able to swallow liquids and talk in a whispery voice.

Then, on December 2, he took a dark turn. He couldn't sit up without his blood pressure plummeting to fifty-nine. When he tried to drink, the liquid went into his lungs. He was moved to hospice care.

On the morning of December 8, ten days short of his seventy-first birthday, my brother told his wife of forty-nine years that today, he was going to die. And he did.

That evening when I called my son to tell him of his uncle's death, he said, "Now, it's just you."

It's just me.

* * *

My brother was cremated, his ashes placed in a sleek black box. After the funeral mass, we followed the procession to the graveyard behind the church where his ashes would be buried beside his daughter's grave. Before we left the church's vestibule, I stopped the priest and touched the box that contained all that was left of my brother—everything we'd shared, everything we might have shared, reduced to ashes—then I cried.

At the funeral luncheon, my sister-in-law leaned toward me and said, "Let's not lose touch."

I nodded yes.

Grief binds us. We text, we call. I share with her memories of my brother and me from our childhood. She updates me regularly about her children and grandchildren.

When I talk about my brother, sometimes people say that he brought on his own fate by never taking care of himself. Or they say, "you were never really close." That only deepens my grief. Why weren't we close? Why didn't he take care of himself?

Like so many people in this book, I'm haunted by legacy and

family secrets, what we inherit, and what is nurtured in us. But, unlike them, I've always known the heavy burden of our family's addictive tendencies.

In the end, was my brother powerless to kick his addiction to cigarettes because of our family history of addiction? Or was the compensation of cigarettes too lovely to leave, to loosely quote the poet Richard Hugo?

Alcoholism and addiction run in my family tree on both sides. My brother could never kick his nicotine habit. My father almost died from alcoholism, only to succumb to throat cancer from a lifetime of smoking a pipe. My mother's sister became addicted to prescription pills. The list goes on and on.

"Gail, there's always at least one alcoholic in every generation of our family," my great Aunt Catherine told me at my father's funeral.

Was that a warning or a kindness? Or both?

Because I knew my family legacy, when my children were teenagers, I told them of our history of addiction. I knew too well that nobody in the family escapes alcoholism unscathed, whether you're the child, the spouse, or the alcoholic. I didn't want that to happen to them.

The question that still haunts me is: *Did I fail my brother?*

In the chaotic house we grew up in, it was me, his older sister, that he came to for comfort, which I gladly gave. In adulthood, it wasn't as easy as holding him while our parents argued and criticized. Somewhere along the way we became untethered from each other.

Since we were never close, and because I feared upsetting our newfound relationship, I never asked him how he felt about our Black heritage—another opportunity lost.

Knowing my brother as I did, if it had troubled him, I'm certain he would have told me. I want to believe that he took my mother's lessons of tolerance for all people to heart. At least that's what I tell myself.

Goldfish Crackers
Sunday 3/26/23
For my brother

Not bread crumbs but goldfish,
bleached by sun and rain—
a path I have no choice
but to follow, as if there's a way
back. The scent of things
seen, the way death comes.

Four months now, I wait for dreams—
you speaking, who had so much
to say, now silent.

Goldfish like childhood,
ours together forever gone
only me left remembering
how we were once
upon a time.

CHAPTER 25

Strangers Keep Telling
Me Their Secrets

Marriott East, Louisville, Kentucky

March 2023

As the hotel elevator descends, I feel the nervous energy pulsing in the small space. There are four of us, one man and three women. Glancing at their lanyards, I know their names and their states: OHIO, IOWA, COLORADO.

I also know that each of them harbors a family secret they have brought here to Untangling Our Roots—the first-ever summit to unite adoptees, donor-conceived people, and non-paternal event people (NPE).

The elevator jerks to a stop. A woman enters: COLORADO.

She, too, scans everyone's lanyards. Her eyes finally rested on a blonde woman in her thirties wearing chic athletic wear as if she's ready for anything life throws at her.

Pointing at the woman's lanyard, she says, "You're from Colorado, too." Then she puts her hand on her heart. "I'm an adoptee. What about you?"

"Donor conceived," the other woman answers as easily as if she'd been asked "where did you get those clothes?"

I'm jarred by their frankness, but not surprised. After all, isn't that why they're here? To share their common experiences of misattributed parentage?

My journalist brain is in full tilt—the book ever-present with me. I want to ask them how they found out. DNA results? Or had a parent finally told the truth in a moment of emotional stress?

But the elevator doors open, and they disappear into the large cacophonous room's miasma.

As I make my way through the throngs of people to my author table, dragging my suitcase of books, my *White Like Her* poster under my arm, not for the first time I realize in some ways that I'm an interloper. My parents are my birth parents, but I do have a family racial secret, which I'll be discussing at tomorrow's author panel: "Loss and Unknown Roots."

Even though I haven't had a misattributed parental experience, in a way, I've become a repository for others' family secrets. Emails from strangers continue to ping my inbox—some asking for help, some just wanting to be heard.

Last month, I received an email from a man who tells me that he looks white and that his birth certificate says he's white, but, like me, he's mixed race. His sixth great grandmother was an enslaved woman from South Carolina. As if he knows I'm writing this book, he ends his email encouraging me to keep writing.

Many more stories to tell. And many more secrets to hear.

Today will be no different.

I share my author table with Christine Jacobsen, the author of *Dancing Around the Truth*. We hit it off immediately. No need for small talk. We both have written books about our racial surprises. Through a DNA test, Christine discovered the man who raised her wasn't her biological father. Her biological father was a Black dancer from the Bahamas.

We sell books, chat with people who wander by our table, the afternoon wanes. Christine leaves, and I'm about to do the same.

Suddenly, as I'm packing up, a woman is standing in front of my table. Maybe in her mid-thirties, though I'm a terrible judge of age. Brown hair, casually dressed. There's an edge to her.

Her lanyard is twisted, so I can't see her name or what state she's from.

"You're the reason I came," she says emphatically. "I wasn't going to come, but I saw your name. I drove here from central Illinois."

From the intensity of her gaze, the way she leans in, her hand resting on one of my books, I sense she desperately wants to tell me something. I'm both pleased, but wary. My mother's story sometimes elicits unexpected emotional reactions from people.

The woman's gaze drifts away toward the DNAngels booth as she gathers her thoughts. I wait.

Then she looks at me and begins to tell me her story.

"Two weeks ago, I got my DNA results. Shocker: My dad's not my dad. I asked my mom about it. At first, she wouldn't tell me. Then she did. It happened while she was separated from my dad. She had an affair with this guy she knew. She thought she couldn't get pregnant. I guess she was wrong. I'm just glad my dad's no longer here."

"Do you know who your birth father is?" I ask. After almost two years of interviewing people who've had these parental discoveries, the question comes easily.

She scoffs. "It's a small town. I know who he is. As soon as I found out, I marched over to his house, knocked on his door, and told him I was his daughter. He told me to leave and not come back. End of story."

Her mouth is tight with anger and hurt.

"I'm sorry," I say. Of all the people's stories of parental discoveries I've listened to, none of them were so recent and so raw.

"Look, I'm a business woman. I run my own travel agency. People work for me. I can handle this."

She pauses.

"I'm not sure if I'm going to stay. I just wanted to meet you."

"You might want to stick around and check out some of the panels," I offer believing that the panels might help her.

"I don't know. Thanks anyway."

I Thought I Could Handle This

It's the second day of the summit, late in the afternoon. There's a line of people waiting to buy my book. Probably because they attended my author panel.

The line starts to dwindle. I look up after signing a copy of my book and see the woman from yesterday. She waits until everyone leaves.

"I thought I could handle this. But I can't."

She starts to cry.

I hold her hand while she cries. There's nothing else I can do, except to say, "It's good that you stayed."

From my own discovery experience and from listening to others with similar experiences, I know the difficult journey that lies ahead for her, as she begins putting the pieces of her identity back together. As I hand her my card, I tell her to email me via my website if she wants to talk. I never hear from her again.

When I think about the stories in this book and the bravery of the people sharing them, I think about what the novelist Sigrid Nunez said at the end of her novel, *The Friend*: "What we miss—what we lost and what we mourn—isn't this what makes us who, deep down, we truly are."

From these splintered pieces of who we once thought we were, we heal and forge our new selves.

ACKNOWLEDGMENTS

My heartfelt thanks to the courageous individuals who trusted me with their stories. In particular, I owe a debt of gratitude to Kara Rubinstein Deyerin who contributed to my research and was my liaison with several of the NPEs in this book. Her tireless advocacy for genetic identity rights is truly inspiring.

I'm most grateful to my dear friend and colleague, Linda Landis Andrews, for reading a draft of the book. Her savvy and thoughtful suggestions helped shape the book, and her encouragement kept me going through the rough patches.

Thanks to my editor, Jesse McHugh, for shepherding the book through an exacting edit at a particularly difficult time in my life, and to everyone at Skyhorse Publishing for their continued belief in my work. Many thanks to my literary agent, Jill Marr, for encouraging me to write a follow-up book to *White Like Her*.

This book would never have come to fruition without the unflagging support of my husband, Jerry—my safe harbor, my life partner, and my best friend for more than fifty years.

RESOURCES

Right to Know: www.RightToKnow.us.

Untangling Our Roots Conference: https://untanglingourroots.org.

Watershed DNA: https://www.watersheddna.com.

DNAngels: https://www.dnangels.org.

Donor Conceived Community: https://donorconceivedcommunity.org.

NAAP—National Association of Adoptees & Parents: https://naapunited.org.

Reunion Land Reads offers additional reading on DNA surprises, adoption, and donor conception: https://bookshop.org/shop/reunion landreads

Severance Magazine—has a comprehensive list of resources sorted into categories: https://severancemag.com.

Jodi Klugman-Rabb, PsyD, LMFT. LPC, Psychotherapy, Pioneer, Parental Identity Discovery. https://www.jkrabb.com.

ENDNOTES

Chapter 1

1 *MIT Technology Review*, "More than 26 million people have taken an at-home ancestry test." Antonio Regalado, February 11, 2019, Accessed March 7, 2024, https://www.pewresearch.org/short-reads/2019/08/06/mail-in-dna-test-results-bring-surprises-about-family-history-for-many-users/.

2 Ibid.

3 Libby Copland, *The Lost Family*. (Harry N. Abrams; Reprint edition, June 1, 2021) 144.

4 Ibid, 217.

Chapter 2

5 Gail Lukasik, *White Like Her: My Family's Story of Race and Racial Passing* (Skyhorse Publishing), 15.

6 Ibid, 18.

7 Gail Lukasik, "My mother spent her life passing as white. Discovering her secret changed my view of race—and myself." *The Washington Post*. November 20, 2017.

Chapter 5

8 Alvin J. Tillery Jr., CSDD & 23ANDME RACE AND GENOMICS SURVEY. August 17, 2018, accessed February 2, 2024, https://csdd.northwestern.edu/research/csdd-23andme-race-and-genomics-survey-2018.html.

9 Ibid.

10 Darcel Rockett, "Skin Color vs. Identity: How Americans View Race 'a Huge Surprise.'" *Chicago Tribune*. September 30, 2018.

11 Ibid.

Chapter 8

12 Leslie Alexander and Michelle Alexander, "Fear" in The 1619 Project, ed. Nicole Hannah Jones (One World, November 16, 2021), 117.

13 David Wright Falade, "Mixeded: A son's story," *The New Yorker*, July 11 & 18, 2022, 20.

Chapter 9

14 "XY Chromosomes," reviewed by Psychology Today Staff, *Psychology Today*, accessed July 18, 2023, https://www.psychologytoday.com/us/basics/x-y -chromosomes.

15 Peter Boni, *Uprooted: Family Trauma, Unknown Origins, and the Secretive History of Artificial Insemination*, (Greenleaf Book Group Press, January 25, 2022), 181.

16 Georgina Lawton, *Rootless: In Search of Family, Identity, and the Truth About Where I Belong*, (Harper Perennial, New York, 2021), 270–271.

Chapter 11

17 Katie McLaughlin, "5 things women couldn't do in the 1960s," CNN, August 25, 2014, accessed August 26, 2023, https://www.cnn.com/2014/08/07/living /sixties-women-5-things/index.html.

Chapter 12

18 Ellen Herman, "A World War II Soldier Seeks Information about his Background, 1943," The Adoption History Project, accessed February 12, 2024, https://pages.uoregon.edu/adoption/archive/WWIISSIAHB.htm. Source: Letters to and from Ruth Brenner, October 5, 1943. October 25, 1943, and November 6, 1943, Viola W. Bernard Papers, Box 160, Folder 6, Archives and Special Collections, Augustus C. Long Library, Columbia University.

19 Ibid.

20 Ibid.

21 Ibid.

22 Ellen Herman, "Confidentiality and Sealed Records," The Adoption History Project, accessed November 22, 2023, https://pages.uoregon.edu/adoption /topics/confidentiality.htm#:~:text=The%20intentions%20behind%20 confidentiality%20were%20benevolent%2C%20but%20sealed,reform%20 movement%20that%20gathered%20steam%20in%20the%201970s.

23 Elizabeth J. Samuels, "The Idea of Adoption: An Inquiry into the History of Adult Adoptee Access to Birth Records." *Rutgers Law Review* (Winter 2001) 367-436. Accessed February 15, 2024. https://scholarworks.law.ubalt.edu/cgi /viewcontent.cgi?article=1478&context=all_fac.

24 Ellen Herman, "Confidentiality and Sealed Records," The Adoption History Project, accessed November 22, 2023, https://pages.uoregon.edu/adoption /topics/confidentiality.htm#:~:text=The%20intentions%20behind%20 confidentiality%20were%20benevolent%2C%20but%20sealed,reform%20 movement%20that%20gathered%20steam%20in%20the%201970s.

25 Ellen Herman, "Confidentiality and Sealed Records," The Adoption History Project, accessed November 22, 2023, https://pages.uoregon.edu/adoption /topics/confidentiality.htm#:~:text=The%20intentions%20behind%20 confidentiality%20were%20benevolent%2C%20but%20sealed,reform%20 movement%20that%20gathered%20steam%20in%20the%201970s.

26 Ellen Herman, *Kinship by Design: A History of Adoption in the Modern United States*; (The University of Chicago Press, December 1, 2008), 62.

27 Ibid.

28 Ellen Herman, "Confidentiality and Sealed Records," The Adoption History Project, accessed November 22, 2023. https://pages.uoregon.edu/adoption/topics/confidentiality.htm#:~:text=The%20intentions%20behind%20confidentiality%20were%20benevolent%2C%20but%20sealed,reform%20movement%20that%20gathered%20steam%20in%20the%201970.

29 Ellen Herman, *Kinship by Design: A History of Adoption in the Modern United States*; (The University of Chicago Press, December 1, 2008), 122.

30 Ellen Herman, "Confidentiality and Sealed Records," The Adoption History Project, accessed November 22, 2023, https://pages.uoregon.edu/adoption/topics/confidentiality.htm#:~:text=The%20intentions%20behind%20confidentiality%20were%20benevolent%2C%20but%20sealed,reform%20movement%20that%20gathered%20steam%20in%20the%201970s.

31 Ellen Herman, *Kinship by Design: A History of Adoption in the Modern United States*, (The University of Chicago Press, 2008), 129.

32 Ellen Herman, "Telling," The Adoption History Project, accessed February 18, 2024, https://pages.uoregon.edu/adoption/topics/teling.htm.

33 The Baby Scoop Era Research Initiative: Research and Inquiry into Adoption Practice, 1945-1972, "What was the 'Baby Scoop Era'?" accessed February 18, 2024, https://babyscoopera.com/home/what-was-the-baby-scoop-era/.

34 Ann Fessler, *The Girls Who Went Away: The Hidden History of Women Who Surrendered Children for Adoption in the Decades Before Roe V. Wade*, (Penguin Books, New York, 2006), 43.

35 Ellen Herman, *Kinship by Design: A History of Adoption in the Modern United States*, (The University of Chicago Press, December 1, 2008), 149–150.

36 Ann Fessler, *The Girls Who Went Away: The Hidden History of Women Who Surrendered Children for Adoption in the Decades Before Roe V. Wade*, (Penguin Books, New York, 2006,) 36.

37 Libby Copland, *The Lost Family*. (Harry N. Abrams; Reprint edition, June 1, 2021), 129.

38 Ellen Herman, *Kinship by Design: A History of Adoption in the Modern United States*, (The University of Chicago Press, December 1, 2008), 149–150.

39 Abigail Lindner, "Adult Adoptee Access to Adoption and Birth Records: History, Controversy, Legislation and Societal Change," National Council for Adoption website, accessed February 23, 2024, https://adoptioncouncil.org/publications/adult-adoptee-access-to-adoption-and-birth-records-history-controversy-legislation-and-societal-change/.

40 Nancy Verrier, *The Primal Wound: Understanding the Adopted Child*, (Gateway Press Inc., 1993,) xvi.

41 Ibid, 1.

42 Paul Sunderland, "Life Works: Dedication to Recovery," YouTube video, 2011, accessed on 11/15/2023, https://www.youtube.com/watch?v=3e0-SsmOUJI.

43 Ibid.

44 "What is the History of Adoption?" Adoption Organization, May 29, 2019, accessed March 17, 2023, https://adoption.org/what-is-the-history-of-adoption.

45 Paul Sunderland, "Life Works: Dedication to Recovery," YouTube video, 2011, accessed on 11/15/2023, https://www.youtube.com/watch?v=3e0-SsmOUJI.

46 Nancy Verrier, *The Primal Wound: Understanding the Adopted Child*, (Gateway Press Inc. 1993,) 92–93.

47 Marcy Axness, Ph.D., "The Primal Wound: Separation Trauma IS Trauma . . . At Any Age," accessed November 18, 2023, 5, https://marcyaxness.com/adoption-insight/primal-wound-separation-trauma/.

48 Bastard Nation, accessed February 19, 2024, http://bastards.org/thank-you-for-visiting/.

49 Ilga.gov, Public Act 096-0895, accessed March 11, 2024, https://www.ilga.gov/legislation/publicacts/96/PDF/096-0895.pdf.

50 GOV.UK, "Accessing your birth records," accessed February, 23, 2024, https://www.gov.uk/adoption-records.

Chapter 13

51 John Simerman, "Legislature weighs parole eligibility for longest-serving inmates: Bill would grant parole eligibility to life prisoners convicted before 1973," www.nola.com, April 25, 2022, accessed January 22, 2023, https://www.nola.com/news/legislature-weighs-parole-eligibility-for-longest-serving-inmates/article_d1ee2f90-c4e5-11ec-b383-9bdb288b24c0.html.

52 Ed Pilkington, (New York), "Louisiana ordered to remove teens from 'intolerable' conditions at state prison," *The Guardian*, September 2023, accessed March 19, 2023, https://www.theguardian.com/us-news/2023/sep/11/louisiana-angola-prison-teens-conditions.

53 Gina Miranda Samuels, PhD, University of Chicago, "'Being Raised by White People'; Navigating Racial Difference Among Adopted Multiracial Adults," *Journal of Marriage and Family*, January 27, 2009, Wiley Online Library, 80-94, accessed January 22, 2023, https://onlinelibrary.wiley.com/doi/epdf/10.1111/j.1741 3737.2008.00581.x?domain=p2p_domain&token=ZCNB2ZN4WNFJSPF2UXID.

Chapter 14

54 Verda Byrd, *Seventy Years of Blackness: The Autobiography of Verda Byrd/Jeanette Beagle*, as told to Joyce Garlick-Peavy, (Harrison House Publishing, 2017), 11–17.

55 Ellen Herman, "Confidentiality and Sealed Records," The Adoption History Project, accessed November 22, 2023. https://pages.uoregon.edu/adoption/topics/confidentiality.htm#:~:text=The%20intentions%20behind%20confidentiality%20were%20benevolent%2C%20but%20sealed,reform%20movement%20that%20gathered%20steam%20in%20the%201970s.

56 Ellen Herman, *Kinship by Design: A History of Adoption in the Modern United States*, (The University of Chicago Press, December 1, 2008), 123.

57 Verda Byrd, *Seventy Years of Blackness: The Autobiography of Verda Byrd/Jeanette Beagle*, as told to Joyce Garlick-Peavy, (Harrison House Publishing, 2017), 10.

58 Ibid.

59 Ellen Herman, "Transracial Adoptions," The Adoption History Project, accessed February 27, 2024, https://pages.uoregon.edu/adoption/topics /transracialadoption.htm.

60 Verda Byrd, *Seventy Years of Blackness: The Autobiography of Verda Byrd/Jeanette Beagle*, as told to Joyce Garlick-Peavy," (Harrison House Publishing, 2017), 30.

61 Ibid, 18.

62 Avianne Tan, "Adopted Woman Raised as Black Finds Out at Age 70 That Her Birth Parents were White," *Good Morning America News*, June 24, 2015, accessed February 24, 2024, https://abcnews.go.com/US/adopted -woman-raised-black-finds-age-70-birth/story?id=31997402.

Chapter 15

63 Jack F. Rocco, MD, *Recycled: A Reluctant Search for True Self Through Nurture, Nature, and Free Will*, (Ingenium Books Publishing, Inc., June 18, 2023), 28.

64 Ibid, 8.

65 Ibid, 97.

66 Ibid, 105.

67 Ibid, 179.

Chapter 16

68 Ann Fessler, *The Girls Who Went Away, The Hidden History of Women Who Surrendered Children for Adoption in the Decades Before Roe V. Wade* (Penguin Books, New York, 2006,) 72.

69 Ibid, 134.

Chapter 17

70 Britannica, "Artificial insemination in humans," reviewed and updated by Robert Curley, former Encyclopedia Britannica editor, accessed December 4, 2023, https://www.britannica.com/science/artificial-insemination.

71 *Newsweek*, Science, "'Ghost' Fathers: Children Provided for the Childless," May 12, 1934. 16.

72 Ibid.

73 Ibid.

74 Philip Bloom, MB, ChB, "Artificial Insemination (Donor)." *The Eugenics Review*, 48 (1957), 205–207.

75 Ibid.

76 Ibid.

77 Peter Boni, *Uprooted: Family Trauma, Unknown Origins, and the Secretive History of Artificial Insemination*, (Greenleaf Book Group Press, January 25, 2022), 95.

78 *Newsweek, Science,* "'Ghost' Fathers: Children Provided for the Childless," May 12, 1934. 16.

79 Brian Clowes, PhD, "The Early History of Assisted Reproduction," *Human Life International,* June 4, 2020, accessed December 2, 2023, https://www .hli.org/resources/history-of-assisted-reproductive-technology/

80 *Time,* "Medicine: Artificial Bastards?", February 26, 1945, accessed December 20, 2023, https://time.com/archive/6782908/medicine-artificial-bastards/.

81 Peter Boni, *Uprooted: Family Trauma, Unknown Origins, and the Secretive History of Artificial Insemination,* (Greenleaf Book Group Press, January 25, 2022), 228.

82 George J. Annas, "Fathers Anonymous: Beyond the Best Interests of the Sperm Donor," *Family Law Quarterly,* 1980 Spring; 14 (1): 1-13, https: //pubmed.ncbi.nlm.nih.gov/11665146/.

83 *The Guardian,* "People born by egg or sperm donor in UK will be able to find out biological origins," September 18, 2023, accessed December 5, 2023, https://www.theguardian.com/society/2023/sep/19/egg-sperm-donor -uk-find-biological-origins-anonymity-law.

84 Lucie Jourdan, Director, *Our Father* (Netflix documentary film), Blumhouse Productions, May 11, 2022.

85 Lindsay Lee Wallace, "Netflix's Our Father Tells the True Story of a Fertility Doctor Who Used His Own Sperm on Patients," *TIME,* May 12, 2022, accessed December 19, 2023.

86 Molli Mitchell, "'Our Father': What Happened to Dr. Donald Cline and Where is He Now?" *Newsweek,* May 11, 2022, accessed December 18, 2023.

87 Right to Know, "The Fighting Fertility Fraud Act of 2023," accessed November 29, 2023. https://righttoknow.us/fertility-fraud-laws/.

88 Peter Boni, *Uprooted: Family Trauma, Unknown Origins, and the Secretive History of Artificial Insemination,* (Greenleaf Book Group Press, January 25, 2022), 218.

89 Mary Whitfill Roeloffs, "Doctors Impregnating Patients: Major Cases In 2023 Allege 'Fertility Fraud' Lead To 'Secret Children.'," *Forbes,* December 15, 2023, accessed December 18, 2023, https://www.forbes.com/sites/maryroeloffs /2023/12/15/doctors-impregnating-patients-major-cases-in-2023-allege -fertility-fraud-lead-to-secret-children/?sh=6232f6d74d58.

90 Jacqueline Mroz, "Fertility Fraud," *New York Times,* March 6, 2022.

91 Amanda Pfeffer, "Disgraced fertility doctor agrees to $13M settlement with families, including 17 'Barwin babies,'" CBC News, July 28, 2021, accessed December 28, 2023, https://www.cbc.ca/news/canada/ottawa /disgraced-fertility-doctor-norman-barwin-1.6232776.

92 Right to Know, "The Fighting Fertility Fraud Act of 2023," accessed November 29, 2023. https://righttoknow.us/fertility-fraud-laws/

Chapter 19

93 "The Evolution of the American Family Structure," CSP Global, July 10, 2020, Concordia University, St. Paul, MN, accessed January 9, 2024, https://online. csp.edu/resources/article/the-evolution-of-american-family-structure/.

94 Who Are You Made of? "Ancestry DNA: Close Family," accessed January 7, 2024, https://whoareyoumadeof.com/blog/ancestry-dna-close-family/.

Chapter 20
95 Ann Fessler, *The Girls Who Went Away: The Hidden History of Women Who Surrendered Children for Adoption in the Decades Before Roe V. Wade*, (Penguin Books, New York, 2006).

Chapter 21
96 "Erin's Law—What is it? Training, Curriculum," Recreated by Attorneys Against Child abuse, accessed December 6, 2023, 2023, https://www.erinslawillinois.org.
97 "What is Identity Diffusion? Definition and Example," ThoughtCo., accessed December 9, 2023, https://www.thoughtco.com/identity-diffusion-definition-examples-4177580.

Chapter 22
98 Ann Fessler, *The Girls Who Went Away: The Hidden History of Women Who Surrendered Children for Adoption in the Decades Before Roe V. Wade*, (Penguin Books, New York, 2006), 118.